Jess ...

are happier now than they ever were, because they have evolved a working philosophy for a rewarding, meaningful way of life, the "secret" of which they share with us in this deeply personal and searching book.

- Find the clues to your real self

- Decide your priorities

- Live in harmony with life

- Learn to surrender to life

- Break down your defenses against closeness and love

"The authors reveal their fears and failures along with the triumphs. The program they have worked out, trying to surrender to life as it is and to accept themselves as they are, may encourage others to change self-defeating, destructive patterns."

—*Library Journal*

Fawcett Crest Books
by Jess Lair, Ph.D.:

"AIN'T I A WONDER . . . AND AIN'T YOU A WONDER, TOO!"

"HEY, GOD, WHAT SHOULD I DO NOW?"

(with Jacqueline Carey Lair)

"I AIN'T MUCH, BABY—BUT I'M ALL I'VE GOT"

"I AIN'T WELL—BUT I SURE AM BETTER"

"Hey, God, what should I do now?"

by JESS LAIR, Ph.D.
and JACQUELINE CAREY LAIR

FAWCETT CREST • NEW YORK

"HEY, GOD, WHAT SHOULD I DO NOW?"

THIS BOOK CONTAINS THE COMPLETE TEXT OF
THE ORIGINAL HARDCOVER EDITION.

Published by Fawcett Crest Books, a unit of CBS Publica-
tions, the Consumer Publishing Division of CBS Inc., by
arrangement with Doubleday and Company, Inc.

ISBN: 0-449-23586-6

Printed in the United States of America

First Fawcett printing: October 1975

6 7 8 9 10

For our children and their children with love.

And for Sharon Wike, whose interest, comments, and typing skills made her a part of this book also.

Foreword

So many people have written us asking, "How did you get where you are and what part did your wife play?" This book is our answer. It shows step by step how we went from a heart attack, through heart surgery and other crises, to where we are now. It tells what we were like, what we did, and what we are like now. It tells how we uncovered and developed the ideas in *"I Ain't Much, Baby—But I'm All I've Got."* It shows how, as we have continued on in the development of our ideas, we have moved from a self psychology to the relationship psychology laid out in the last chapter.

Most of all this book is our attempt to tell you our story honestly and to show you how we tried to take our sorrows and use them as stepping-stones to a life of serenity and abundance.

(In this book we will take turns speaking a chapter at a time. The last chapter is a joint expression.)

"Hey, God,
what should I do now?"

_____

1

Jess

"My God, I'm going to die."

This is the thought that is with me so many times every day. For over ten years now, there has been a constant war going on inside me. My fear of death and what desire I have to live are fighting each other and I have a hard time telling which one is winning.

In many ways, though, I now have the kind of life I had always wanted. It's the kind of life I had given up all hope of ever having before I had my heart attack.

I went from a harried, frightened advertising man with no friends and not much family to a college professor in Bozeman, Montana, living in a beautiful log home in a mountain valley with my horses in the front yard, a few close friends, and a family who can stand me—most of the time.

But while I had nothing then and everything now, the war within me still goes on without much sign of letting up. And while I'm healthier now than I've been in twenty years (I even go skiing and elk hunting in the moun-

11

tains), I know that unless I can find more peace than I have so far, I will too often fulfill my own fear and spend part of my time in that living death where fear of dying kills life.

That's why I am working on those problems in me and in my life that brought on the heart attack, plus the problems that arise out of my daily reaction to it. The more I study heart trouble, the more evidence I find to indicate that my heart attack came out of disordered behavior and out of my poor way of handling problems. I feel that even slight changes in the way I live can make big differences not only in the fruitfulness of life, but in protecting myself against literally killing myself.

What's more, I feel that heart attacks are very similar to other physical problems—like ulcers. There are probably many other ailments that can come out of disordered living where we don't yet see the connections clearly, but I think they are there.

A good example of this is the speed with which many men die after they retire. They can't cope with the problems of retirement so they don't want to live and quickly find a way to die. What is interesting is the wide variety of methods they use to die. That wide variety suggests to me that most diseases are not like strangers who come and infect the body, but that their seeds lie within us waiting to be triggered by problems in our lives.

I recently read that one of the cancer-causing agents is something that is in all our cells, usually causing no problem; but then all of a sudden it does. What makes this happen? I think it is possible in some cases that a disordered way of living gradually weakens our body so when a crucial incident comes along, cancer can break out.

There was an interesting report in *Psychology Today* (August 1972) where William A. Green, a psychiatrist at the University of Rochester Medical Center, took a look at sudden deaths due to heart attacks at the Eastman-Kodak plant in Rochester. Nearly all the victims had been "running sad" for some time. Their depression, said their wives and friends, was interrupted by sudden, unpleasant developments in their personal or work lives that made them highly anxious or angry. Heart attacks and death followed quickly.

One of the most common factors precipitating a heart attack was a child's leaving home or disappointing the father's expectations. In one typical case, the father became depressed after the departure of his last child. His wife said later that he had not been able to express his feelings and, according to Green, "compensated by overextending himself by working harder at home or at the plant or shoveling snow vigorously, and developed a sudden cardiovascular collapse."

I think a lot of us are a heart attack or an ulcer waiting to happen. The high cholesterol counts, clogging of the arteries, and other physical symptoms are more a result of a wrong way of living than the cause of the heart attack.

The crucial question then becomes: "Are you and I trapped in the way we live and the things we do?"

Here's where I find the example of Alcoholics Anonymous so encouraging. My friend Vince spent fifteen years on Skid Row as a wino. Yet for the last twenty-three years Vince hasn't touched a drink. At sixty-eight, he has a wife, thirty-five, and five kids seventeen to five. While he could easily have died at forty-five, at sixty-eight he is far healthier than most. But Vince hasn't taken any health cure. He has spent his time cleaning up his stinking thinking and giving up his old ways as he found new and more fruitful things to do.

So we aren't helpless prisoners of our past, doomed to live out some set of self-defeating patterns. We maybe can't change ourselves too much, but we can sure change the things we do.

The ideas that I have found helpful to me are very simple. They aren't easy—they are terribly hard. But they are very *simple*. Many people think something that sounds simple must be easy. Not so. Others feel that if an idea is simple, it must not be any good. Not so. And others try to complicate very simple ideas in order to run away from them. Don't do it. KISS is my way of reminding myself to Keep It Simple, Stupid.

This book is about the program Jackie and I have worked out to find a better way of running our lives. It consists of trying to run them by not running them, by trying to surrender to life as it is and to ourselves as we are in some deep way. It is asking frequently through the day when we face some possible trouble or are in some jam, "Hey, God, what should I do now?"

This is my side of the story of my fight with fear and my struggle to find a life that is more meaningful to me. I'm going to try to tell you my story as honestly as I can because I have seen the life-giving effect on me of the people who have told me their stories openly and honestly. The love they showed me as they told *their* stories helped calm me down and feel less alone. And it helped me see a little deeper into myself and my own story.

This first part of my story I told briefly in another book, but it needs retelling here in more detail.

I was thirty-five, I had a small one-man advertising agency in Minneapolis. I had lunch one noon to discuss with a friend a plan I had been working out over the last year. The plan carefully outlined how I was going to generate $500 to $1,000 a month extra income to be invested in real estate and the stock market. I was going to generate this money by forcing myself to work harder at a business I hated and feared. The purpose of my plan was to generate enough savings in the next fifteen years so that I could retire at fifty and finally do what I wanted to do.

As I tell you about it now, that sounds so absurd that you might have trouble believing it. But absurd or not, that was me. Or at least that was the screwed-up thinking I was doing then.

Well, the deep part of me must have seen the absurdity and futility of what I was planning. On the way back to my office, my heart rebelled. I think my heart said to my head, "Look, you dumb Norwegian head, you may want to go down that sick path, but I'm not going along." So I had a heart attack.

I managed to get across the street to a doctor. I was hauled out of his office on a stretcher, carried to a waiting ambulance, and rushed to a hospital.

As I lay in that hospital receiving room waiting for my wife to come I felt a deep calm. It was as if all my distracting thoughts had been cleared away and my mind and soul could concentrate all their energies. The thoughts and feelings I had in those few minutes are so clear to me, I can still feel them today.

I saw that my whole life had gotten way off the path. It was like coming to a fork in a road and taking the wrong fork, and then another, and another. So finally, I was so far away from where I belonged that there was nothing of the deep me that I recognized in the life I was then leading.

Not only did I see my sick thinking in some big basic choices I had made in life, but I saw its impact in some seemingly little things.

One of the thoughts I had was that my brother, who wasn't making nearly as much money as I was, had a deer rifle and I didn't. I had a huge home and cars and was spending lots of money. But I didn't have the hundred-dollar deer rifle that I had always wanted.

But one of the reasons I didn't have one is that I wouldn't have had time to use it anyway. I was so afraid of my business that I could hardly take a vacation. I was afraid the whole business would be gone when I got back.

I now know it was irrational to worry about it so. Most

of my clients had been with me for three to five years. But most mornings I was sure all my clients would quit me that day.

So even if I would have had a deer rifle, I wouldn't have had time to use it. But worst of all, I wouldn't have had anybody who wanted to go hunting with me anyway. I didn't have any time for real friends. To me friends were something I used. When I wanted amusement I reached for a friend. When I got through with him, I put him back on the shelf and told him: "Wait here and I'll come back and play with you again someday."

As I lay on that cart, stripped of everything, I thought deep and clear for the first time in my life. I realized my whole life was screwed up. I realized I was doing a whole bunch of things I didn't believe in. I found myself saying to myself, "I'm never again going to do anything I don't deeply believe in."

That decision helped my calm. It helped me get through the next few days of oblivion. But the big problem I found in the years since then is how hard it is to find what I deeply believe in. I'm getting a better idea now so I don't sway with every switch of the breeze. But I am still amazed how tough it is for me to know what I believe.

My wife, Jackie, came in soon after I got to the hospital and that memory, too, is as clear as this morning. We reassured each other. But she also helped me with her great directness. I'm continually denying all things unpleasant. When I do, she says of me, "You can sit on a pile of horse manure and call it roses longer than any human I know." Some of her directness must have rubbed off on me because I found myself saying, "You know I could die, don't you?"

She told me, "Yes, I know that," and it was a comfort to have the fact out in the open between us. I still didn't feel afraid. That would come later.

Then Father Howley came. He is as kind and gentle a

man as I know. His concern for my life showed on his face. But that helped, too, because he wasn't trying to hide anything from me. He gave me the last rites of the Church and that made me feel better.

It may have been fortunate I had that time and those feelings because I shortly slipped into an oblivion that was a three-day nightmare of snatches of wild consciousness mixed with long periods of drugged blackness, pain, and struggle.

Jackie said I talked about my business and what had to be done, but I don't remember any of that.

My next memories are of a couple of days of semi-consciousness and people coming and going with great seriousness.

Then one morning I was moved to a room with another heart patient and I was weak but well and conscious. Immediately the hell-raising coronary personality of mine that had helped give me a heart attack showed itself. And the instant calm I had felt for those first few minutes three days earlier left, never to return completely again.

There were six or eight student nurses on our wing of the hospital. I started talking to them. Soon I was having deep, intense talks with them about literature, nursing, and my philosophy of life. Within a day I had set myself up as a one-man university.

I very carefully explained to one rather plump young student nurse how she should increase the breadth of her reading by reading a book in an hour or two rather than by puttering through it, and I gave her the assignment of doing this with a couple of books and reporting back to me.

One lovely student nurse and I had long talks about J. D. Salinger and what he was trying to tell us in *Franny and Zooey*. Some of the young nurses just came in and were cheerful and smiling and lit up the room with their happy ways.

But one of the student nurses and I really managed to

screw things up. I don't remember just what happened but one afternoon she was talking to me about some boy friend problem she had. I said something that she didn't like, so about eleven o'clock, as I was trying to settle down for the night, she came back to my room and told me how angry she was because of what I had said.

So here I was just a few days out of a heart attack in a nice neutral hospital environment and I already had a good fight going when I should have been sleeping. I was trying to solve problems and educate people with my ignorance when I should have been resting.

That hospital experience has always been a good example to me of how much of the trouble around me I cause. And another instructive part of that experience was how near at hand help is.

Jackie couldn't be with me much because of visiting rules and her own problems of keeping herself, our family, and my business afloat. But there was a man of about fifty-eight in the bed next to me who was some kind of saint. His name was Arnie Erickson. He had had a heart attack twenty-five years ago but now he just had some small problem. Arnie had worked out a good philosophy of life and was able to live it pretty well. I can see now that all I would have had to do to solve my self-created troubles in the hospital would have been to let go of my sick games and put myself in the wise hands of my wife and roommate. But I didn't have enough sense to do that. I needed those sick games to take my mind off my problems. And I didn't see the alternative that was so close to me.

What were my sick games? Well, I can't stand peace and quiet. So, when confronted by peace and quiet, I will stir up some commotion. I will create some kind of problem for myself that I can't quite handle. That way my struggle with the problem blinds me to what I am really faced with. In the hospital I used deep intellectual and emotional discussion with the student nurses to avoid thinking about my own problem.

Perhaps you have some of these sick games in your life. Lots of power and glory pushes are just attempts to build up the ego in a false way by putting a patch over it. Lots of drinking and gambling and hell-raising isn't for fun, it is just a way of hiding from ourselves and creating troubles for ourselves so we and the people around us can be preoccupied with those troubles instead of our real selves.

It is terribly hard to give up our sick games when they are the only games we've got and when they serve our interests and our needs. They are much better than nothing.

But I find if we can make ourselves try some good games, we can get some good rewards. But we won't give up that sick game until we see we have something better to take its place. No amount of moralizing will make the wife give up her boy friend. Even if she wants to let him go, she probably won't until she has built something more loving in her relationships with her husband, family, and friends.

So it's fairly easy to see sick games, but it is slow, hard work to get rid of them.

Arnie, my roommate, had one saying that has helped me a lot ever since. He watched one of those student nurses come in the room with a cheery smile and happy talk as she went about straightening up the room. When she left, the room looked nice and we felt good. Arnie's comment was: "Boy, nursing sure fits her like a glove."

When the student nurse who had started the fight with me came in our room, she would try to straighten things up, but would do just the opposite. She would get all the pictures hanging cockeyed. She would move the vases to the edge of the tables where they were in danger of falling off and she would leave the whole room in chaos with her bad disposition and unfeeling ways. When she left Arnie would remark: "Boy, nursing sure doesn't fit her like a glove."

I have held on to that simple idea of Arnie's ever since. I use it as a way of testing if something is right for me or not. Does it fit me like a glove? If it doesn't I see it as a sign something about that thing is wrong for me—and I will put it down.

You can do the same thing in your life. What part of your work do you like the most? What do you do easiest and best? Find a way to make that a bigger part of your job. What part of your work do you like the least and do last? Try to get rid of as much of it as you can. What friends and interests do you like the best? Increase your time with them. Let the other things drop out of your life.

While I was in the hospital a problem came to a head in my business that had been brewing for six months. I was doing business with a crook. When I started working with him I didn't know how crooked he was. I did know his checks weren't good. But I figured that I could deal with him where others couldn't. And I was desperate for the business.

While I was in the hospital my wife went down to the office to see about keeping my business going. She looked in one of my desk drawers and found $5,000 in bad checks from this man. She didn't know that many were duplicates and that there was only $2,000 involved. But either way it was a big problem to her at the time.

And what did my nice crooked friend do? He sent me a big floral piece about three feet wide and two feet high. It must have cost $100. I called it my "duck blind." I'm sure he charged it to his company and some poor florist is still trying to collect.

Eventually it was time for this maniac, me, to go home from the hospital.

My first memories at home were of how scared I was. I was away from my nice safe hospital. I felt like a piece of delicate glass; any false move would make me break all to pieces.

My roommate had told me another good story. It was about what fear can do to you. After he got out of the hospital with his first heart attack in the 1930s, he had to change to easier work. That was at a time when doctors didn't know much about heart attacks and put too much emphasis on taking it easy. Their advice and the fear of some of their patients caused an extreme overreaction.

Arnie told of selling Watkins products door to door. Once in a while he would run into a heart attack victim. He would be sitting in his bedroom slippers in an armchair in front of the living-room window. He was so afraid to move that he was hanging onto the arms of the chair as if the chair was life itself. And, of course, we know now that he was doing the very thing most likely to kill him.

By giving in to his fear and spending his whole time sitting waiting for a bad signal from his body, he almost ensured a reoccurrence of his problem. But even worse, the minute he sat down in that chair and gave up hope, he guaranteed a living death for himself by making his life meaningless.

The heart attack victims like me, who overreact with action at least get some exercise. Like anything else, of course, the happy medium is somewhere in between.

So, here I was at home feeling as fragile as a crystal goblet. My family was happy to see me but scared stiff about what to do with Dad. I sat in my easy chair and they all sat and stared at me. To break the strain, we watched "Car 54, Where Are You?" That night the show was one of the funniest they ever had. Muldoon got into a problem with some love-starved blonde and I laughed till I cried, so hard I nearly died. At least, I was afraid I might die and just the effort of my laughing scared my family.

My wife had moved our big, king-sized playpen of a bed downstairs into the dining room so I would not have any stairs to climb. The next problem I was faced with was going to bed. All doctors have sex lives like monks so they have no trouble keeping a straight face when they tell their patients not to have intercourse for at least six months after a heart attack. I have a feeling most of their patients (except the most frightened ones) don't wait that long. Intercourse is then a fearful experience.

They are now finding out some things about intercourse I hope the doctors will be quick to pass on to their patients. I read of one study recently where they wired typical middle-aged heart patients with an EKG sending device which transmitted the EKG to a monitoring station. The patient kept a diary of his activities. By comparing the diary and the EKGs it was determined that sexual intercourse causes only a moderate elevation in the EKG and that elevation lasts for only a short time. The only really dangerous intercourse was when it was outside the family. The extramarital intercourse caused some very extreme reactions in the middle-aged male's EKGs.

You'll notice in the above, I said "typical." I am not a doctor and I cannot and must not presume to give medical advice. Only your own doctor can advise you. I mention this study only to show that by middle age the physical demands of intercourse aren't quite as great as some of the sexual athletes down at the gym would suggest. But then, big talk has always been cheap.

One interesting development I found a few days after I got home was that I was finally going to get to know my wife. We were married on a Thursday and both went to work the next Monday. That was our honeymoon. Our longest vacation had been a week and we always had kids along or we were with friends. But now we were faced with weeks, even months, together. Thank God we were reasonably compatible. We had the basis for talking together and we had a common concern for our family unit, which was the one thing both of us valued most. By family, I don't mean only our children, I mean the whole unit, which includes my wife and me.

I find in talking to my students and the people who come to me for help that they often have bad feelings about their families. But as they work on their feelings toward themselves, their feelings toward their families change. And they tell me, "Jess, my family changed toward me." Well, they didn't. Most of our families are waiting to love each other and us. Usually we aren't giving them a chance. I find our families are often a much bigger and better resource than we are willing and able to see at first.

In my case, my wife wanted me to live. So did I. We started to think about what we were going to do. She thought maybe I should get out of my business. She was ready to sell everything to help me make a change if that was best.

For once in my life I really listened to the people who loved me. An advertising client who was also a friend of mine said I should consider teaching. My kindly neighbor across the street also thought I should get out of business. He said I didn't have any "killer instinct." I think what he meant was that I wasn't concerned enough about the process of making money to be a good businessman. I wanted to have money but I didn't enjoy the process of making money.

So we decided to sell the house, the sports car, and the business. I called a former college classmate and asked if he wanted to buy my business. He bought it the next day. We put our house on the market and sold it at a good price. We even sold a bunch of smaller things that seemed so necessary when I bought them, but didn't seem so important when I started looking at life differently.

Think how nice you would feel to get rid of some of

the things that are weighing you down. I had made much bigger mistakes than most, so had much more weighing me down. But any lightening of the load is a help.

During all this time my wife acted as though giving up the beautiful home we had worked so hard twelve years for was no problem for her. It must have been. I had been poor as a kid. All I was used to was eating regular and a minimum of comfort with an occasional luxury here or there like a raisin in a cake. But my wife had been used to being well off. What we had was the way she and her friends expected to live. So it must have been terribly hard for her to go along with the drastic changes in our life even though she didn't show it. Not only did she go along, she actually led in urging the changes.

At one point we hesitated about selling the house. We thought I could go back to school and we could continue to live in our high-powered suburb, the richest in the United States in terms of average income per family. But we thought better of it and realized we had to make a break with the past.

Since then I have seen many wives of heart attack victims who seem to say to their husbands, "You go back to your job and do just what you did before, even if it kills you, so we can continue to live just the way we have." That's death to me. Even if the job the guy is going back to is okay for him, that wife's attitude of business as usual seems to me to be dangerous and destructive. I think what marriage there was got worse or even died, and I think the guy won't live so long and the years he does live will be unhappy ones. Much more often, though, the wife wants the husband to cut the standard of living and he is the one who won't do it.

A heart attack seems to me to be usually two things. It is always sorrow and grief. It is also something we can use as a means of growing in our lives. If we don't, it kills our spirit. There is no way we can run away from it. We must pick up that cross and carry it—or it kills us. So it is grow or die.

A heart attack is a cry for us to examine our life and see how living out of tune with life might have helped cause the attack. In some cases, a heart attack might be purely a genetic accident due to factors completely beyond our control. But in any case we have to come up with some new way to live in response to our heart attack so that we can get the most years possible from life, and even more important, so we can learn to make the best use of those years to make sure they are full, not empty.

Time is a funny thing. I had my heart attack at thirty-six. My five kids were from two to twelve years old. My hope was that I could live long enough to see my youngest son's children. That would mean about twenty years of life. I now see that years aren't nearly as important as what we do with them.

I used to spend lots of time waiting for time to pass. And in those times, the clock seemed to go so slow. It was like the clock in school on a warm spring day. It seemed as though three o'clock would never come. But the funny thing was, the years were empty and they went by so fast. Lately, I've noticed a nice thing. My days are so full of things I like and enjoy that every time I look at the clock I'm amazed how fast time has gone and so many things happen in a day. But because the days are so full now, a year lasts forever. The twelve months seem like an eternity. So now I'm a lot more interested in taking care of my days than in how many years I'm going to have.

I think that if you try some of these things, you can lead a much fuller life, too. I say that not only because these things have worked for me, but because I've seen them work for so many.

There is a part of my story you need to know to be able to make any sense of how I got things so screwed up and some of the things I did to regain some sanity in my life.

I was living the way I was because I was trying to prove to a bunch of people in a small town in southern Minnesota that I was really something. That doesn't make much sense unless you know something about what happened in Bricelyn, Minnesota, and how I reacted to it. If you asked me to sum up in one anecdote how I felt in response to those years in my life, I would tell you about a church picnic I went to in Fairmont, Minnesota.

Each summer the Baptist church in Bricelyn had a picnic. That summer we went to Fairmont. I must have been thirteen or fourteen. I had gotten hold of a fly rod earlier and had done some fly fishing. In most ways we were quite poor, but in other ways we had some very fancy things, like a Packard convertible that a movie star used to drive.

At the picnic, I was walking by an old car and I looked in and saw a fishing outfit with a cheap rod and a cheap tin reel and I thought it was one of the most pathetic things I had ever seen. I still remember that scene and the feeling in my stomach. I remember feeling a horror at ever having to live like that. It may sound ridiculous to react so strongly to such a simple thing. But it's like clouds parting suddenly and revealing the mountains they hide for just an instant and then closing again. That incident revealed to me a deep part of my character—or lack of it. I was, at thirteen, already desperately needing fine things to show the world what I was. And I was already horrified at any blemish on any of the things that I used and surrounded myself with to define myself.

What happened there in that little town that could make me pour my life down a rathole for fancy things? What gave me such overdriven strivings and helped me have the earliest heart attack in my crowd? I still don't know very well, but I have some ideas. But you need to know what went on there to see where that heart attack and screwed-up living might have come from. And you need that background to understand better the struggle I'm still making today. It's my past and I'll explore it with you when it is my turn to speak again. I don't blame my past. It's like one of my young students said to me, "For what I am today, shame on my past—but if I stay that way, shame on me."

2

Jackie

"Are you Jackie Lair?"

"Yes."

"I'm Miles McNally, Jess's insurance man. I'm awfully sorry. Jess has had a heart attack and I'm to take you to the hospital."

Who is this insane person? What in God's name is he talking about? Jess is at work. Jess is only thirty-six. We have five children. Jess can't have a heart attack, he can't die. I can't take care of the kids alone. My God, he has to be wrong. I won't listen. I'm going to black out. I'll run.

In an instant's time these were my thoughts. My legs buckled and I pitched forward for an instant, then drew a deep breath and squeezed three-year-old Joe's hand tighter.

I was in Minneapolis. My mother-in-law, "Grandma Bertha," had slipped on ice the previous day and broken a bone in her shoulder. I had driven Grandma downtown to see the doctor and had taken Joe with me, leaving eighteen-month-old Mike with my cleaning lady.

In the doctor's office, Joe had started to fuss so I took him out for a Coke. After that we had walked over to Donaldson's Department Store to buy Grandma a robe that would slip easily over her broken shoulder.

Now, I am stepping off the elevator to return to the doctor's office to get Grandma, and here is this man.

Miles McNally. Oh yes, I've met him before. What is he trying to tell me? Jess has had a heart attack. A heart attack? Heart attack means death. No. Jess is only thirty-six. He won't die. He can't die. I love him. I need him.

Joe. What will I do with Joe? Give him to Grandma. My God, Jess is Grandma's son and it's her son who has had a heart attack and she's got a broken shoulder. I've got to see Grandma.

I stepped into the doctor's office and asked for Grandma. A pretty, unsmiling face floating above a white dress opened a door. There was Bertha. She looked so small and calm. "Bertha, I have to go to the hospital to see Jess. Can I leave Joe with you and we'll get you home some way, and then I'll get my mother to take the kids?" I'm so short of breath and my mouth is so dry. Grandma looks up and says, "Yes." Not a tear, not a grimace.

"I'll let you know how things are when I get to the hospital."

As you can see, I was in a state bordering on shock. I am sure many of you have had this experience.

What happens to us when death or near-death comes like a bolt of lightning?

I've read a lot of articles about how the adrenals marshal their forces in times of stress and send many excess secretions flowing into our systems to prepare us for "flight or fight." I was glad to have the nervous energy they supplied, but I found the heart-pounding, short-of-breath, dry-mouth feeling rather frightening.

My thoughts raced on.

Miles and I entered the elevator. I've got to call my mother. Into the car. Whose car? My car is here. Jess's

car is downtown, too. No, I can't drive. We'll send someone for the cars. I got into Miles's car and we started for
the hospital. What hospital? Swedish Hospital. I've never
seen the inside of Swedish Hospital. What's Jess doing at
Swedish Hospital? I must have said these last words out
loud because I heard Miles's voice saying, "Jess had his
heart attack in his office and he called me. I told him to
call Dr. Duryea, who is my doctor. His office is right
across the street from Jess's office." Later I learned that
Jess called Dr. Duryea and told him he had chest pains.
The doctor asked him how he was feeling now and Jess
said all right. And so Jess *walked* over to Dr. Duryea's
office. He didn't walk out of *his* office, though. He rode in
an ambulance!

An ambulance. My God, Joe and I had walked right
past Jess's ambulance with its doors open and its lights
twirling. I remember thinking, "Someone must be pretty
sick."

We arrived at Swedish Hospital and walked up to the
desk. I heard Miles's voice asking for Jess's room
number.

Eleventh floor.

We walked over to the elevator.

I am not prepared to face the eleventh floor yet. Some
phones beside the elevator—I know, I have to call my
mother about the kids. I stepped back. Miles stared at me
as if I was insane.

I've got news for him. I was!

"I've got to call my mother about the kids." I fumbled
for a dime.

"Hello, Mother, Jess is sick. He's in the hospital. Will
you go over to my house and get the kids? I don't know
what's wrong, he might have something wrong with his
heart." I hung up. Now who could I call? No one. I finally stepped into the elevator.

As many of you have done or will one day do, I not
only had to deal with heart disease on this day of days,

but I had to cope with a strange hospital, doctors I had never heard of, and I was soon to hear a whole string of foreign-sounding words which are the peculiar language of disease.

The extra adrenaline, or whatever, that was coursing through my body with a force that I could physically feel was doing its job. I walked and I talked—I functioned.

I was having wild, uncontrolled thoughts. My thoughts would light quickly on Jess, then jerk painfully to our children. In another split second a wave of physical feeling would roar through me as reality tried to find a perch in my mind. I wasn't ready for reality yet. My ungoverned brain would not settle down.

I don't think the good Lord intends that we take all trauma into ourselves and understand it in an instant. He sends a special chemistry into our bodies that dulls one part of us as it quickens another. I'm sure you've seen this type of thing happen.

I had physical things to do, I had to see Jess, I had to function physically for yet a while, as my mind continued its disjointed race.

I walked down to the end of the hall on the left. Here's the door. I have to go in. Miles stepped back. I have to go in alone. It was a big room. Lots of windows. Who is that stranger on the bed with an oxygen mask on his face? That's Jess. It can't be. Yes, it is.

"Hi, Jess." I fumblingly reached for his hand. I was afraid to touch my own husband. I touched him and he looked up. He pulled off the mask, and smiled. My God, he's as gray as putty.

"You know I might die, don't you?" he said.

"Yes."

Now, what a stupid thing to say. I can't think of anything more to say. Jess is turning over. He grabs the phone. He dials. My God, he's calling Jim. (Jim is our friend first, our attorney second.) Jess is yelling something about a will. Oh good, here's a nurse. She'll settle

Jess down. The nurse carries a hypo in her hand. She asks me to step out of the room. How stupid. Jess is dying, she's going to give him a shot, and I have to step out of the room as though there was something obscene about that cute little fanny I know so well.

Out in the hall I realized I was glad to be out of that room. In fact, I never wanted to go back to it again.

How confusing to have thoughts like that. How many of you have been horrified at some thought like this that seems contrary to what one should be thinking?

Ah—a phone. I've got to talk to someone. Someone I know. Someone who'll understand how frightened I am. I'll call Phyllis. We know each other well. We have shared our joys and our sorrows. Phyllis went through many a session with me a few years back when having a child with cerebral palsy and four others—one after another— had led me to a psychiatrist's office. She'll know I can't take this.

"Phyllis—Jess has had a heart spell."

"Where are you?"

"I'm at Swedish Hospital. Eleventh floor. Call the Hoffmans—they're our neighbors. Tell them for me. Call Father Howley. Tell him. Oh my God, Phyllis, I don't know what to do."

"Just hang on, Jackie. I'll call them for you and then I'll come down when I get the children settled for the night."

Night? What time is it? It's four-thirty in the afternoon. Jess had his heart spell at one. I heard about two-thirty. Is it only two hours? Heart spell. Can't I say heart attack? No. No one has told me anything but Miles. I won't say it until I hear it from the doctor. Doctor? I haven't seen the doctor yet. I'd better go back to Jess's room. Down the hall, end room on the left.

I pushed open the door. Jess was lying flat on his back all covered up. He had the oxygen mask on his face. I tiptoed up to the bed. He's asleep. Or is he dead? I looked at the blanket on his chest. Wow—it's moving up and down. He's alive.

The nurse came and told me to come down to the waiting room. "Jess needs his rest and you will be more comfortable down there." How dare she call him Jess? She doesn't even know him. Why do nurses always try to separate you from people you love?

I remember when Janet was born. She was born with an encephalocele. This was a malformation of her spine, at the base of her brain. I was twenty, Jess twenty-three. I left the hospital without even touching my first-born. When she was ten days old the pediatric surgeon called and said her condition was such that they must operate in the morning. Jess and I knew that she might die in that operation. All I wanted was a chance to hold her in my arms.

My mother called the hospital and told the nurse that I would be in very early so that I could hold Janet.

I got to the hospital early, but Janet had been removed. She lived, and I got to hold her. But the anger and frustration I felt at the hospital personnel who were playing God with my emotions was still very real.

And here I was again—being told what to do by a spooky nurse in a white dress.

I submit. I never was a fighter. Down to the waiting room. Oh God, where are you? It's so lonely in this paneled room. In this leather chair. I look down on the lights of the city. It is dark and snowy and cold. What time is it? Why don't I ever wear a watch? I must have three at home in my drawers somewhere. Look at all the traffic. All of those men going home to their families.

Why wasn't I a better wife? Why did I get so angry at Jess for being so busy all the time? Why wasn't I stronger? Maybe if I hadn't bugged him so much about how hard it was to take care of the house and all the children. The house. Why, why did we move to Edina? I could have said no. We didn't need a new house. And my

Triumph. I didn't need a sports car. Why did I just stand there and let him buy and buy and buy. I have so many "things" and now I might not have him.

Guilt was ever present in the first few days.

I feel that guilt of this type is predominantly a woman's disease. I call it the "mother's syndrome."

How many of you read and reread all of the " How to Raise Your Children" and "Are You a Good Wife?" articles that have been so abundant these past few decades? Don't they invariably cause twinges of discomfort?

Now, in the present time, after ten years of intensive living and learning I have come to realize: We all are imperfect beings. We live in an imperfect world. We all do the best we can, most of the time. Sometimes, in my case, I do a great deal less than my best.

I finally wearied of my guilt enough to set it aside. I was using it as a shield. I no longer have need of that crutch.

You are surprised that I use the word "crutch"?

Through the years I have found that any tool, good or bad, that I use to keep me from facing the fact that I am a limited human being, and cannot change the universe, is a crutch.

For my serenity I need to see myself in perspective.

How much better we would all feel if we stopped our attempts to control our worlds.

My thoughts continued on that long-ago day:

He's such a lonely, frightened guy. Why couldn't I have helped him more? I know he is stupid not to see how talented he is. Why didn't I help him understand how foolish he is to worry, instead of getting impatient with him? No more. God—if he lives through this I am going to help him find himself. I'm going to be a positive force in his life instead of a negative one.

But damn damn damn. He is stupid. I love him, but for a smart guy he sure is dumb. He doesn't know how to relax. Relaxing to him is going over to the health club and lifting weights for two or three hours. He's so damn tired from running around town all day, and then he pushes himself even further by running over to the health club after supper. He won't watch TV. He won't read much. He has to run, run, run.

He wasn't always like this. When did it start? No. He *was* always like this. Remember, hunting, fishing, golf, poker with the boys, skiing, visit people, run to the store, do this, do that.

Remember putting in the garden? To me it involved planting a tree and dropping six seedlings by the back door. To Jess it meant moving the right half of the yard to the left half of the yard and building a terrace and shoveling and sweating from Saturday morning till Sunday night.

How about the driveway? To me it was a truckload of gravel spread out thin with a rake. To Jess it was three truckloads of gravel—ankle deep—that must be moved from one end of the drive to the other by the wheelbarrow load.

It's just his nature to work hard.

How many of you have husbands like Jess? I have, in the ten years since Jess's heart attack, talked to women numbering in the hundreds who feel an instant bond when I describe my Jess. How many of us are there?

Hey—who is this? Ah. Jim, Jess's brother. They sure do look alike. Jim wants to see Jess. Oh—do I have to take him down the hall? Yes—I do. I took a deep breath. Here we go. Down the hall. Peek in the door. Are the blankets still going up and down? Yes. Okay, we'll go in.

Jess roused and smiled at Jim. Jim, rough, tough Jim, is choked with emotion. Jess closes his eyes and Jim and I flee back to the waiting room.

I'm so glad someone is here. One by one friends and family drift in. Miles is back. Or has he been here all the time? I don't know. I don't ask. It's funny how all of this attention helps me to get through this.

"Jim—our cars are still downtown, can you get someone to help you get them home?"

Jim leaves to move cars. I think he is relieved to have something to do.

Why haven't I seen a doctor yet? I had, but I had forgotten. Dr. Duryea had met me outside Jess's room. He told me Jess had some abnormalities on his EKG. I didn't understand what he was talking about. I had never seen him before and forgot him two seconds after he left.

I found that I was functioning on many different levels. I spoke to the doctor. I asked questions. I listened to answers. But the overwhelming shock of the situation demanded that a part of my mind close up like a tight fist. This closed-off part of my mind accepted only what it was ready to accept. I spoke to the doctor, I heard what he had to say, then my mind stored this information in a dark recess to be recalled when and if I was ready for it. In the meantime, I functioned on a surface level.

My family arrived. I looked at their familiar faces as though they were strangers. I had nothing to give them. I was stripped of emotion. While their very closeness demanded response, I greeted them as one would a distant neighbor in the supermarket. All surface, no depth. I had no energy to spend.

I was frugal. They were kind.

I think they knew they could not intrude into my agony. I was alone though surrounded by people. Thus it has ever been for fragile humans. But in this fragility lies strength. Husbanding resources buys time. And as we all know, time *does* heal.

Who is this man in the white coat? He is Oriental. He's asking for me. He has such an accent I can't understand him. Miles understands two words. Myocardial infarction. Miles looks at me. "Well, he's had the big one." Big one what? Heart attack. That's what. Heart attack. That thing that kills old men. That thing that happens to other people. It's happened to Jess.

"What time is it?"

"Eight o'clock."

"Did you eat anything, Jackie?"

"Eat? I don't remember."

More people drift in. My father asks me why I don't go down and see Jess. I can't. I don't want to leave this brightly lit room full of healthy people for that room at the end of the hall with a stranger in it. A man who left for work only twelve hours ago, healthy and vital. Now he might be dead and I don't want to peek in the door and find out. As long as I am here seeing my friends, talking to people, I can push the horror of my thoughts away.

Here's Father Howley. He is carrying a little black pouch in his hand. Oh—the last rites. Extreme unction. I smile. I shake his hand. We walk down the hall together. Through that damn door again. Jess is awake. Father says he's here to give Jess a sacrament. Jess nods and smiles. He's calm. Good. Father opens his leather pouch. The oils and other things necessary for the last rites are there. Father looks around at the walls. There is no crucifix on the wall.

"This is Swedish Hospital, not St. Mary's, Father." Father asks me for my rosary beads. I fumble in my purse. I know the beads aren't there. I haven't carried them for years. But Father assumes I have them and I haven't the nerve to say no.

"Hey, Father, I don't seem to have them in this purse."

No matter. Father asks me to step out while he hears Jess's confession. Now what would Jess have to confess? He doesn't have a mean bone in his body. I've never seen him knowingly hurt a soul.

I step back in. Jess receives Communion. Father begins to anoint Jess. His eyes, his ears, his feet. Look at how blue and cold his feet are. He could die. But I don't think he will. He's young. We love him. Peace. Peace is coming. Jess goes back to sleep. Father and I leave.

Religion and its rituals meant a lot to most of us when

we were children. As we grow up many of us sadly leave much of this behind.

I went through a period of seeing ritual as silly superstition. A period of believing there was no God. I was beginning to mellow as many of us do in our thirties and forties. I hadn't found my way back to full acceptance at this time, but I found the age-old forms and rituals of Catholicism comforting in their familiarity. I was deeply comforted by the hope that there was benefit in the ceremonies.

And lo, with that small shred of hope my mind began to settle.

I remember as a child reciting catechism, rattling off the trio—"faith, hope, and charity." I never understood or thought about the meaning of those words. I think all too few of us recognize the tremendous power of that one word: hope.

I find, and I am sure you do, too, that as long as there is hope, I can fight. I can survive.

How I have come to love and fight for the hope in any incident or situation.

Don't tell me anything is hopeless. Without hope, many of us curl up and die. We must have hope.

The frantic feeling is gone. I smile and chat with friends and family. Jim returns from his car shuffling. Everyone is tired. It is time to go home.

I am not going home. A kind nurse gives me a pillow and a blanket. I lie down on a couch. Someone is on the other couch. Is it Phyllis? I think so. I sleep for a few hours. It is 1 A.M., my brother Tom is here. I peek at Jess, then Tom takes me home for a quick shower and a change of clothes. The house is so dark and quiet. The children are at Mother's. Grandma Bertha is at Jim's. I shower and change. I think I will drive my own car to the hospital. Then I can come and go without bothering anyone.

Oh dear God. We are the same people we were yesterday and yet—and yet—we will never be the same again.

I am alone at the hospital now. I peek at Jess. He's still asleep. Yes, the covers are still going up and down. I retreat to the lights of the waiting room. I think and think: If only I had done this, if only I hadn't done that. Regrets, recriminations, guilt. I would have a lot of that in the weeks to come. And then anger, too. As if Jess could have stopped his heart attack if he would only have taken life a little easier. I was thinking grossly selfish, angry thoughts one minute. Then the next minute I would feel a rush of sympathy and tenderness for him lying there in that hospital bed.

And so the first night passed.

And the next.

And the next.

Monday. Jess got sick on Friday. I haven't been home except for a shower and clothes. And I have to go down and open his one-man office. I can't. I've never worked in my life. I don't know anything about advertising. I can type. I can spell. But what I do best is cook and wash clothes and wipe babies' noses and bottoms.

Deep breath. Off the elevator. Smile. Don't let anyone know you're scared. Into the office. Look at his messy desk. Papers piled everywhere. Work work work. No wonder he had a heart attack.

Open the drawers. Find the client list. Start calling them one by one and tell them what has happened. Bill Holbrook and Mary Ellen Olson. They have a travel bureau. They're old friends as well as clients. Mary Ellen was widowed at the age of twenty-two. She'll understand. I call them. They are shocked. They will help in any way they can. On down the list. Everyone is wonderful. But what help can they be? I don't understand what Jess did for them. I don't understand how to place advertising. Lord knows I couldn't write an ad if Leo Burnett himself stood there and helped me. (Leo Burnett owned one of the largest advertising agencies in the world. Jess worked for the agency in Chicago for a year—a year that was traumatic and devastating to both of us—but that is another part of our story.)

I think that going to the office on Monday morning brought home to me the awful sense of aloneness that I kept trying to push away. Aloneness and pure blind panic. Everything I was or wanted to be was wrapped up in that body lying at Swedish Hospital. How could I possibly go on if something happened? "Something happened." That is the phrase I chose to use. It's easier than "died" or "dead" or "death."

As I went through Jess's desk I found a thick stack of checks all marked "Insufficient Funds." They were from a client, to pay for advertising that Jess was on the hook for. With a quaking heart I added them up. Over $5,000. Dear God, no wonder Jess is sick. We don't have that kind of money. All of our money is tied up in debts. I picked up the ledger. I tried to figure out how badly this guy had gotten into us. I couldn't figure it out. Then my stout ancestry came to my aid. I picked up the phone and called the crooked SOB. "What are you going to do about the bad checks you've given Jess?"

He softly and sweetly told me not to worry. He'd cover the checks. It wasn't as much as it looked like because some of the checks were to cover other checks. He condescendingly tried to calm down the hysterical wife.

I found this was just more of his lies.

Not a week later I found that he had placed some advertising for his company in the Minneapolis *Star* and *Sunday Tribune* and charged it to Jess! So much for him. I swore I'd get him if it took me a year. I found out "hell hath no fury" like me. Luckily, Jess's contract with the newspaper had run out the previous week and we could not be held responsible for this man's advertising. I was happy to let him try to fight the Minneapolis newspapers.

By the end of the day panic and exhaustion had set in. I knew I couldn't handle the children, the house, the hospital, and the business, too. Since the business was impossible for me I knew I had to get help there. How? I did a very feminine thing. Jess would never think of asking one of his clients for help, but I didn't hesitate a minute. I piled a lot of papers and contracts into a briefcase that was on the floor. I walked out the door, locked the office, and drove over to Bill Holbrook's house. In my exhaustion and naivete, I walked into Bill's home and asked him to take over Jess's business until Jess could get back to work.

The fact that Bill and his partner Mary Ellen Olson were clients of Jess's with their travel bureau, Americans Abroad, didn't matter at all. I asked the impossible. Bill and Mary Ellen, God bless them, did it. I never set foot in Jess's office again. Bill somehow—I never asked—moved all of Jess's files and equipment from downtown Minneapolis over to Dinkytown. (Dinkytown is a small business section nestled up against the Minneapolis campus of the University of Minnesota.) The only contact I had with Jess's business after that was to collect the somewhat over $2,000 Jess's shifty client had taken from us.

Tuesday, I returned to the hospital and found Jess alert for the first time since Friday and tremendously interested in whether he was going to have a bowel movement or not. Aha! If Mr. Regular can find nothing more to worry about, he's on his way back. I decided it was time to get the children from my long-suffering mother and start putting our life back together. Three of them had school to get back to and Joe and Mike needed their mother.

That night, our first night together without Dad, was difficult. I set the table in the dining room and we all sat down in our usual places with himself's place conspicuously empty. This was too much for Jess Howard Lair, age nine. We called him Howie to avoid a Junior. After fidgeting in his chair for a few minutes, my black-haired little eminence picked up his plate and marched to the head of the table. As he climbed into his father's chair he looked at me and said, "I'm sitting here 'cause I'm the oldest boy and from now on I'm not called Howie, my name is Jess!"

From then on he was my "Man" around the house. My irresponsible, happy-go-lucky little boy felt his father's illness deeply. And a man he tried to be.

One morning I awoke at 6 A.M. to the scrape of a snow shovel. Jess, Jr., was shoveling the driveway. I wept. He's so little and he's trying to be so big. How frightened he must be. He wasn't a boy to talk about his feelings, even then. He just did what he thought he should do. He wanted a lot of hugs and kisses in those days, but no talk! He's still that way—as a grown man.

The girls, eleven and twelve, went their own self-contained way. They chatted about school and friends and clothes, but not about Dad.

Joe, age three, who was with me when we heard about Jess's heart attack, instantly became the king of all thumbsuckers. He never took his thumb out of his mouth for years to come. This resulted in hundreds of dollars' worth of braces for his teeth. Joe also had difficulty in talking and with school in the next few years—but I'm getting ahead of myself.

Michael—age eighteen months—became a lap baby. He was responding to the tension in the house more than to any knowledge he had at his young years.

And so the days went. Children off to school, visit Jess, home for the children. Alone at night. Those were the bad times. But, Jess was going to come home. And soon.

In the evenings I'd think about our life and what we needed to do. Jess had wanted to go back to school and had talked about it over the past few years. How could we swing it? I knew one thing for sure. The house and the sports car would have to go. Like Tevye and his wife in *Fiddler on the Roof,* I had the happy ability to accept the truth when I saw it. And just as they looked at their home when the pogrom came and were able to say, "Who needs this run-down place?" I could do the same. Who needs a house in Edina? Who needs a sports car? And as Tevye and his wife could pile their belongings on a horse cart and start the long trek across Russia to find a home in America, so too did I have that lucky ability to walk away. Who needs it? I've got Jess. We're a family. That's all that counts.

Here I want to say something just to the wives of heart attack victims or potential heart attack victims.

There are a lot of us around. Each year in the United States over a half million people die of heart attacks or heart-related diseases. Many or most of these people are men. Somewhat less than one third of the people who have heart attacks die. So, rounding off figures and allowing for women who have heart attacks, there must be close to a million of us who face "heart trouble" with our husbands each year.

Recently my husband was interviewed on television concerning one of his books.

Jane Johnston, the female half of a Minneapolis television team, asked Jess if it was hard on his wife to give up so much in order to change our lives.

Jess answered, "No, most women would do the same."

Many women reacted angrily to this; they felt that Jess was putting me down.

He wasn't, dear ladies. What he was saying is that most women, if given the chance, would choose having their husbands rather than having "things."

We all know this is true to a certain extent. Yet, I have had to face the fact that I liked "things" and I sent messages to Jess in many devious ways that a nice home, a car of my own, a cleaning lady, private schools for the children, a weekly trip to the hairdresser, nice clothes— all of this was important to me.

I met a young woman in Bozeman not too many days ago. Her husband had had a heart attack. They had given up the big-city rat race and moved to our smaller town. She talked animatedly about how much all of this had meant to her.

"We are together now. We enjoy our children. We live in a run-down old house, but I like it."

As she talked, I came face to face with myself. I found myself thinking: "If you like your new life so well, why are you stressing so hard how fancy your pre-heart attack home was? Why is your voice becoming so tense? Why are your arms waving around so wildly?" I was pained, both for this lovely young woman and for that side of myself that I still show to people that make me feel shy and insecure.

And I found myself remembering all the times I had entertained people at parties by talking about the contrast in our "before" and "after" life. Many times I made us sound wealthier than we *were*, and poorer than we *are*, just for a smart aleck effect.

Jess has listened to me talk that way. What messages has he gotten?

There is a price we women pay when our husbands are struck down that often is as devastating to us as our husband's illness is to him. I think this fact must be faced. The sooner the better.

I recommend trying to face it sooner so that you may be spared the psychological illnesses and nervous traumas that I had to face and am still facing, although to a lesser degree, each day. I feel badly, looking back over the past ten years, to see that for many of those years I stumbled blindly along, not facing certain truths, overreacting to other truths, and all in all, adding to our problems rather than helping.

Jess is coming home! I'm scared. How do I treat him? Will he be okay at home? I want him home. But—I don't want him home. What would I do if he had another heart attack? What if he dies in bed beside me? Yuch—what does a person do when he dies? Does he say, "Wife, I'm going to die," and then turn his head to the wall?

Ha, I know Jess. He'll probably want to go hiking in the snow the day he gets home. The doctor says walking a little each day is good for Jess. Does he know Jess doesn't know what "a little" is? And furthermore, he can't be told. Jess can't take the stairs yet. Okay, call Al Hoffman and have him get our bed down in the dining room. Oh boy, I'm scared. How must Jess feel?

Al and Doc White, our friendly dentist, came and moved the bed. Much fun and ribald remarks about how fellows with heart attacks mustn't have too much excitement. It was fun. And tomorrow I go and get Jess. I didn't know what I felt: Oh boy! Or: I'm scared! A little of both, I'm afraid.

We came home. Jess white and thin. Myself hyper and talking incessantly. Jess hasn't realized yet—after all our years together—that sometimes my mouth and my brain are two completely disassociated entities. I talk non-stop about home, children, snow, traffic, family, etc. and my brain is saying, Watch out. Take that corner carefully. He's full of blood thinners. Accident now and he'll bleed like a sieve from every orifice. Uh-oh, he just took a funny breath. My God, he's not going to stop breathing on the way home! Here's the last turn. Up Maloney Road. Then park in front. Holy cow, we made it home and he isn't dead yet. Now the stairs into the house. "Dear God, don't let four steps kill him now. I can't deliver a dead man to his children."

"Look out, here comes the tribe . . . Watch out, Dad's weak."

"Mike, don't kick Dad." He's full of Coumadin and a kick might start a bruise and maybe he'll bleed to death in his leg before I know it. "Lord, you know I'm not up to this. Why, oh why did you have to pick on us? Wasn't there some nice senile old grandfather you could have given the heart attack to?"

Soon it was time for supper. I had to learn a different way of cooking. Low cholesterol diet. That means no more deep-fried shrimp. Less cheese. U.S. Good meat instead of Choice. And watch the blood thinners. Jess has to go to the doctor's office for a pro-time every week. That's a test of some sort to find out how thin his blood is. We ate supper in shifts in the kitchen. No more dining room. I fed the children and then Jess and I ate. I'm relaxing a little and Jess is happy to be home.

Jess, the TV hater, is on the davenport watching TV with the children. I can't believe it. I think I'll sit down too. I'm so tense every bone in my body aches. Good, here's "Car 54, Where Are You?" We all love that show. Look at Jess laugh. I haven't seen him laugh in weeks. This is a funny episode. Muldoon is getting involved with a girl. This has got to be the funniest one ever. Look at Jess laugh. Wait. He's laughing too hard. He can't stop laughing. Tears are running down his face. He's doubling over. He's clutching his chest. Can a man die from laughing too hard? I'm scared. Stop laughing. I'll turn the TV off. No. Sit still. Good Lord, is this the way life is going to be? Afraid even to laugh too hard? He's okay. I'm glad that program's over. Funny or not.

And so to bed. As I come to this part of the story, now ten years later, I can still hear my mother saying, "A lady does not speak of secrets of the boudoir." Well, there's no help for it. I'm flesh and blood and other women must be wondering how one feels about having intercourse with a husband who has had a heart attack. I know my children will be shocked to hear that Ma and Pa even think of sex still.

The very first night Jess was home I cuddled up next to him and put my arms around him. "Thank you, God, for sending him home. Now, if you'll just cool down my thoughts I can go to sleep and leave this poor guy alone."

The doctors say no. Our hormones say yes! Having no will power we went ahead. Scared? Oh boy, was I scared. He lived. I questioned him carefully. "Any chest pains?"

"Nope."

Okay. We're together again. Things are just about normal.

Since that first night, which was great partly because of long abstinence, we have found that some of Jess's medication does cause a decrease in desire and that it sometimes take a little longer to "get going."

Of course part of this is because we're not as young any more. But I have found that sex "after heart attack" is just about as it was "before heart attack." As the gamekeeper in *Lady Chatterley's Lover* says, "You have to take the thick with the thin."

If we are happy and relaxed, all is well. If we are tired and tense, all is not well. But, as far as fearing heart trouble, our thoughts rarely go along that line since the first few days at home.

As the days spread into weeks, spring came. Spring in Minnesota is a delight. In April the grass started to green up. The trees began to bud, and a fly or two started to buzz against the windows. Time to sell the house. I pushed hard for selling the house, the extra car, and the business. My feminine logic told me that if the ideas all came from me, then Jess could have the option of saying yes or no without feeling he was depriving his family. I pushed hard and Jess was happy to think about going to school.

We sat down with a map of the Twin Cities and surrounding area. With a protractor we drew a circle around the whole area, which gave us an idea of what cities were covered within a thirty-mile driving distance of the university. We both wanted to move to the country. One big reason was old farmhouses were renting cheap. And the less we had to pay for a house big enough for seven of us, the better.

The little black Triumph TR3 with the shiny red upholstery sold immediately. I prayed to God the house did as well.

It didn't. It took time.

My daily prayer was, "Okay, God, you know we need out from under this load. This is a good house. We're not asking too much. Send the right person to us. Come on."

A dear couple, a husband and wife real estate team, were pushing hard to sell our home. We had known each other previously. They have known illness in their own family. Because of their own troubles, they had that wonderful quality that suffering can bring, empathy. They felt our pain.

With their help, our home sold in time. We received sufficient funds from the sale to look more cheerfully toward our future.

Jess sold the business easily. It would afford us a small income for a few years.

And so we were winding up one kind of life and preparing to step out into another totally different.

3

Jess

Why did I have the feeling that I was so far away from what I believed in when I had my heart attack? As near as I can see, the main reason was that I was determined to convince "people" that I wasn't the dirt they thought I was. Who were those people and why did I feel they thought I was dirt? The answer to that lies in a small town in southern Minnesota—Bricelyn.

I could describe my early childhood one of two ways. I was part of a close-knit, loving family clan, which was rare even then. The small town I grew up in had as strong a sense of community as most anything I've heard of in America. So in many ways it was like the ideal child-rearing environment we have heard described. And it was something like the Zululand I talked about in my earlier book. Most of the strengths I have I feel I owe to the things that were given me in that small community.

But that wasn't a perfect society by a long shot. It was as good a society and culture as any I've seen but it wasn't perfect. When you dump an imperfect being like me into an imperfect society there are bound to be some points of stress. And it is those points of stress that can kill me if I don't do something about them.

My accomplishments come mainly from my strengths though they are often made necessary by my weaknesses. But it is my weaknesses that cause the emotional part of my problems and I think they are what eats at my heart.

I read recently of a small community in Pennsylvania that seems the closest to what an ideal community can be in the United States. Not surprisingly, it is an import.

A long time back a large group of Italians settled in this community, which because of prejudice and other factors was forced in onto itself like the Jews in the ghettos. Their common religion and culture was the continuing basis for their community. Even though there is now a wide range of incomes and occupations, the families stayed together. They have their clubs where the garbage man socializes with the stockbroker. And always there is warm-hearted help from the community not only in times of joy and sorrow, but most importantly, in everyday living.

The interesting thing about this community to me is the lack of heart trouble there. The men are big and fat and eat all the wrong foods, yet there are hardly any heart attacks. I think the depth and range of close emotional relationships in that community keep them from heart attacks. And, of course, even more so, these relationships keep the days filled with warmth and life.

This community makes the same point to me that the Eastman-Kodak study I mentioned earlier made. In the Kodak study, the emphasis was on individually disordered lives and how those disordered lives so weakened individuals that a hard blow was fatal.

In this Pennsylvania community I see the ingredients that it takes to make people reasonably happy. The rich, emotional relationships nourish the heart. And when trouble comes, as it always does, the husband and wife are surrounded by real friends who can spot the problems and help overcome them.

The Irish Brother heart study tried to find why the Irish brothers who came to this country died faster than their brothers who stayed in Ireland. There were many surface, detailed reasons for the dying, like changes in eating habits, increased stress, etc. But I think the fundamental reason is that heart attacks are the American disease. I think they reflect our separation and isolation from one another. I grant some other countries have a similar problem. But what I'm trying to figure out is why *my* life in *this* country doesn't make me want to live more, and I can find plenty of very fruitful ideas to work on.

Please understand me. I'm not blaming our society or my family or my past for anything. I simply want to see what was good about it and use it as well as I can. I want to see what was bad about it for me and get away from that as much as I can. All societies I have studied are imperfect at serving the needs of their people. They are imperfect because they were created by imperfect people and are constantly being changed by imperfect people as they react to ever changing conditions.

But I also see that as an individual I can build my own community filled with the people I love and who love me. These people who recognize and act on their need for each other can sustain and make rich each other's lives. That's what I'm doing here in Bozeman, Montana, I'm building that community for me and my family. I'm trying to do in a personal way what those Italians did in Pennsylvania. And I'm trying to remedy some of the defects I saw in my otherwise good life in that southern Minnesota town.

When I speak to my young students of my need for community they see that I'm also implying they need a community, too. Many of them argue against my ideas. That's fine. Any society I have studied has had people who needed their communities and people who were wanderers for part or all of their lives.

I have been a wanderer. I would move my family for $500 more salary and leave my friends and my family's friends without a tear. I have been part of a couple of communities since my heart attack. As to choosing between being a wanderer and being a part of a community, I like being part of a community best.

But I see that most people who talk about making that choice don't really have one to make because what they tell me about their communities says to me they aren't really in that community. People think they are in a community because they live there. Not so. Being part of a community is a very deep, personally involving thing that I'm just beginning to realize after five years here. It means making a real commitment to my community.

Let me show you what I mean by telling you about something that happened last spring. I had taught two of the Real Bird boys in my classes. Henry Real Bird had been to our house often and thought of me as a white brother. Henry's father had died about ten years earlier. Henry told me one day that his mother and little sister and brother were coming to Bozeman to cook for the International Fair. I said, "Good." He said, "They are going to stay at your house." I said, "Good." That was in the winter. In the spring I was invited by Henry's older sister to come down to the Crow reservation to speak.

The afternoon before I spoke, Coey Real Bird came to our motel and invited my two youngest boys and me to go riding. The Real Birds own a piece of land where the tepees sat at the battle of the Little Bighorn. My family went to the Real Bird house and we saddled horses. We rode back of the house to the Little Bighorn and forded where the Indians had a hundred years earlier. We rode up the banks onto the Custer battlefield, myself, my two sons, and the five Real Bird boys.

Our family had visited the battlefield many times. To

us it is a very special place because so much history is there. When I go there I can feel the ghosts, hear the bugles and battle cries, and see the Indians swarming through the hills.

But now I was there in a different way.

As the Real Birds rode with us over the battlefield, my son Michael told them how much he liked Tex, the beautiful sorrel horse he was riding. He was just eleven, but he was a good rider and the horse was just right for him.

When we got back from our ride, Richard, the oldest of the Real Birds, said that he wanted to give Tex to Mike. I said that it was too much. He said no it wasn't too much. Look what I had done for his two brothers.

My boys and I could hardly believe what we were hearing. Tex was one of the most beautiful quarter horse thoroughbreds we had ever seen. Our horses at home were just common-looking horses.

I wish my story could end on this happy note, but it doesn't.

The next morning I spoke to the Indian and white mental health workers. At noon we invited the Real Birds to have lunch with us at the Sun Lodge Motel. I asked them if they were still sure they wanted to give us Tex. They said they were sure. Then they started talking about what a high-priced horse Tex was and how they had been offered $500 to $600 for him. I knew what they were saying was true and I couldn't stand it. I didn't want to be obligated that much. I didn't want to feel that involved. So I said a terrible thing. I said, "Yes, I know what a good horse he was and is, but he has a bad back." As TV's Maude says, "God will get you for that." And I deserve anything I get.

But the Real Birds weren't too disturbed at my white man's ways; at least they didn't show it.

The next week Mike and I drove down with our horse trailer to pick up the horse. I found Richard in the stands watching the enactment of Custer's Last Stand. I sat with

Richard, Chester Medicine Crow, and Johnny Old Coyote. Richard asked me if I had come to get Tex. I said, "Yes, if you still want to give him to us." He said, "What do you think I am, an Indian giver?"

When we went to get the horse Richard touched on the subject of giving. He said, "When we say to someone, 'you are my brother,' we give something to show we really mean it. It is easy just to say 'you are my brother.' But it is not easy to back up those words with a real gift."

That incident when we were given a horse confirmed many things I had been working on and it taught me some new things. But one of the most crucial things it confirmed was one of the reasons I had come to Montana. My roots were in Montana because my grandparents were pioneers there. I vacationed there often. I wanted to live in a smaller town, one I could be more easily a part of. And I wanted to teach where I wouldn't lose all my students to anonymity. In Montana there were only 700,000 people in the state and I figured half my students would stay in the state.

So, here, five years after I moved to Montana, the giving of the horse said I was becoming part of the Bozeman and Montana communities. And the gift was so magnificent that for all our lives Mike and Joe and Jackie and I and the rest of the family will remember that we were the ones to whom was given a horse.

The interesting thing is, I have just started to learn what a community means and how it can nourish my heart.

So when people who think they know what a community is just because they live in one say they don't need or want a community, it doesn't mean much to me. They don't know what they are turning their backs on because until they have made a deep, personal commitment to that community, they aren't a part of it.

It is hard to judge communities from the outside, but I sense that in San Francisco there are a number of real communities because in just one day there I saw two; Chinatown, where everyone knows everyone else, and the people who work on Fisherman's Wharf.

I think being part of a real community solves more problems than heart trouble. I think it helps solve other problems like divorce, ulcers, alcoholism, and suicide. So when the people of Montana tell me this is the "Howdy" state filled with friendly people and friendly communities, I have to ask why the divorce rate is the highest in the United States and the suicide rate one of the highest. The idea of Montana as a pastoral paradise is crazy. The percentage of lonely, frightened, alienated people here is greater than in New York City.

The reason I came to Montana was because I had some roots here to build on and my bones were comfortable here. I knew that there were no more friendly people here than anyplace else.

My dad met my mother when he was working in Montana in 1924. She lived on the next ranch and they rode horseback together, and in a year they were married. My dad loved Montana, but some combination of his attachment to his family and the need for work brought him back to southern Minnesota, where I was born in 1926.

My grandfather's father was a pioneer settler in an area in south-central Minnesota, just a few miles from the Iowa line. A number of my grandparents' brothers and sisters lived within ten to thirty miles of us. All but one of my grandfather's children, my aunts and uncles, lived within ten miles of him in the early days. All were farmers.

This was the family my dad returned to. He rented a little house at the edge of town after I was born. When I was about a year and a half old my mother was sitting reading by a gas stove and it blew up, burning her face and setting her hair and clothes on fire. My dad got her outside and got the fire out, but she was terribly burned. The local doctor was sure she would die, but rushed her to the Mayo Clinic in Rochester, Minnesota, where they were pioneering in skin graft work. She spent two years there, returning home occasionally to rest and wait for grafts to heal.

The fire destroyed what little my parents had and it placed a terrible load on their marriage. My mother was so disfigured that people couldn't help staring uncomfortably at her red, scarred face. A woman's precious possession, her beauty, was gone. And her physical and emotional reserves were exhausted. She and my dad were also under the awful burden of a huge hospital debt, which hung over them for the next ten years and made it necessary for most of the material things they wanted to be purchased in the face of the hospital debt.

During the hospital years, my grandparents and my dad's brothers and sisters who were home raised me and my brother, who was born about six months after the fire.

We have all had traumatic experiences like this in our childhood and they are terribly painful. Janov in *Primal Scream* says he can take us back to the early hurt and relive it so it heals. By getting at the real source of our problem, he can free an individual of his neuroses. From what he tells me, I halfway believe he can do it. But the big problem he has is to find and train enough others so we can all have such a benefit. Until this happens, I will try to see my hurt as well as I can and especially its harmful consequences in my life. That way, I can try to avoid letting that early hurt control my life.

I know a part of me wants to scream out "Mommy!" and "Daddy!" and roll on the floor sobbing. But I can't. So I use the program I'm talking about throughout this book to go on with my life in some way more positive than was possible for me before my heart attack.

My dad tried farming for two years but didn't like it or couldn't make it. He moved to town and supported us by using his tractor and machinery to work for other farmers.

We lived a funny life in those days. As I said, in ways

we were very poor and in other ways we were rich. When I was six, my dad bought my brother and me a pony and saddle. Yet, at the same time, the power company shut off the electricity. I cried because I couldn't hear a favorite radio serial, "Skippy," so my dad climbed the pole in the dark and hooked us up again.

On the farm, I had a pony and on Saturday night a nickel to spend. My brother and I would buy a Popsicle early in the evening and each take half. Later we would buy a 3 Musketeers candy bar, which then had three pieces, and divide it up.

In the winter we took cold bean sandwiches to school on some days. I remember a kid who brought sandwiches made with luncheon meat and lettuce. I can still remember the day I traded sandwiches with him and my enjoyment of that fancy lunch on the school steps. After we moved to town we traveled to Montana for summer vacations and during the rest of the year we spent most of the weekends visiting uncles or the grandparents. Yet one time I can remember my dad telling my mother that if he could only get $50 together, we could get through the winter. As a small boy, I remember asking my mother how come we didn't have meat in our stew like the other kids. But at about the same time I remember constantly coming home from school to freshly baked cakes and cookies.

When I was about twelve or thirteen, my dad bought a ten-year-old Packard convertible, and he would let me drive it once in a while. Yet I remember envying some of the other kids the white shirts they wore on Monday which they had worn on Sunday to church. I didn't have a white shirt. (I realize I may have had a white shirt, but those were my feelings. What the reality was I am unable to say.) One winter in eighth or ninth grade, I remember wearing the minister's old suit to school every day.

As you can see, these memories are rather contradictory. What the so-called real truth was I do not know. I *do* know that my memory of these events and the feelings they caused are very real to me still. And it is those memories and those feelings I have to deal with.

If my mother were to tell me I had twenty white shirts and I only wore the minister's suit one day because I wanted to, that wouldn't change anything. In fact, it would make the problem worse because I would have to face how much I had distorted reality.

In school I did well. Mostly I enjoyed it, but in high school, I was doing some things well partly to put others down. I remember the days we would have quizzes in physics. I enjoyed them because I knew the answers. But I also enjoyed asking Mark Hunt and Merton Quelland, my friends, how they did on their tests. They would have to admit they got two or three wrong. Then they would have to ask me how many I got wrong and I could say, "None."

My beloved coach, Arling Anderson, said one of the cruelest things to me. I still remember the day, and the place he was standing, and the way the sun came in the windows on his tweed suit. He said that if Bernice Johnson knew some of the practical things about batteries and other things boys learn before they ever get to physics class, she would be the best student in the class. I still remember the hurt, because I wanted to be best and I didn't want anyone else to be close. Already I needed to beat people so badly, to be number one. What my kindly neighbor said much later about me in business is true. I didn't have the killer instinct in business, but in competitions of other kinds, I have to win and at times I'm afraid I'd even break somebody's leg or arm to win. So it isn't the prize that counts to me. It's the delicious feeling of the winning.

That competitiveness may be a good thing in some ways for some people but for me most of the competitive victories are hollow, and they are often purchased at the price of the people around me. So the killing way I go about competing keeps me from the people I need.

During all these difficult times my dad kept his balance. His basic economic philosophy, I now see, was, "Buy the luxuries and let the necessities take care of themselves." And they always did. We always ate and most of the time well.

My father's sense of giving was one of his qualities I'm still trying to incorporate into my own life. He was always openhanded with what he had. He was ingenious mechanically and built large four-wheeled trailers which he used in his work hauling sweet corn or beets. His friends and acquaintances were constantly borrowing those trailers and not paying him anything for their use. Sometimes they would be brought back broken and he would have to fix them. My mother would scream at him to charge his friends but he couldn't or wouldn't do it.

When he went visiting, he often took a half gallon of ice cream along. It was near the end of the Depression but people were still poor. He knew they would want to serve us something if we came. So he brought enough ice cream so they could be generous givers instead of trying to make a quart go around for six to eight people.

He loved to visit, to laugh, and to tell stories. And he couldn't keep count of when it was his turn to visit someone. I remember my mother saying she didn't want to go someplace because they hadn't visited us. But he would just go ahead. In the case of one of my aunts, I don't remember her ever coming to our house but we visited them regularly. He just knew they were that kind of people. And he didn't let it stop him from seeing his sister and her family.

My dad yelled and hollered a lot and I was afraid of him. When my brother and I, as kids, stole some of his chickens and sold them to buy malted milks, I thought he was going to kill us out of his anger and out of his shame that his sons should be spoken of as thieves.

My mother had a great courage that she still shows to this day. My dad has been dead for twenty years and my mother seems to get younger instead of older. She has a deep sense of fairness and an appreciation for nature which she tried to communicate to my brother and me.

My brother and I spent our early years playing together and periodically fighting each other. But we had family unity and when some other kid picked on one of us he had to fight us both.

Besides my parents, aunts, uncles, and grandparents, there were a few non-related adults in my town who showed me they really thought I was special. My third- and fourth-grade teacher was Aura Kingsley. She loved Indian lore and taught it to me. She took us all over the state on trips in the school bus on Saturdays. She would stand up in the front of the bus with a cheerleader's megaphone and shout history at us. As we went by Traverse-Bois de Sioux, she told us this was where the white man stole the southern half of Minnesota from the Indians. Miss Kingsley believed deeply in me and managed to communicate some of that belief.

Coach Anderson came when I was in eighth grade. I was a terrible athlete, with lots of desire but no coordination. All I did was fall down, or foul someone. But I was team manager and sat by the coach at all the games. He believed in me deeply and that helped.

Ralph Black was our janitor. My dad hunted but only with his friends. So Ralph started me pheasant hunting at twelve. I took Dad's .410 bolt action shotgun to school and went out with Ralph after school. We walked across the football field into a cornfield at the edge of town and started hunting. A pheasant got up in between us, we both shot, and the rooster fell. Right away Ralph yelled, "You got him." I still am sure that Ralph was the one who shot him, but I was half convinced so I took the pheasant home and proudly walked down Main Street with it.

Recently I had a similar experience but this time I was on the other end. I was hunting with two friends and Bill, one friend's son. Young Bill and I were jump-shooting ducks at a bend in a creek. Just as we got there a big mallard jumped up and we both shot. When the duck dropped, Bill yelled, "I got him." Instead of doing what Ralph Black did for me, and saying, "Good shot," I was horrified to find myself thinking, "I hit that duck, not you. That's my duck!" That's a pretty sad thing to see in yourself as a supposedly grown man.

I've told you about most of the good things that happened in that small town. With all those good things, why did I come out of that town feeling so put down? I still can't say. Maybe there's no background so good that we don't have problems. Maybe what life is about is having to find things out for ourselves. Whatever the case, I remember some deep feelings of being very second-rate in that small town. And I can see now that I can't blame anyone else for those feelings. They were my problem.

I see that it is very common for us to feel second-rate, so that we need ego patches, like big houses or Cadillacs we can't afford. But until we see this need openly we are a prisoner of it. When we see it, we can give up the sick games and get some well games going so we aren't such captives of these feelings.

When it came time to date, I went with the preacher's daughter during my freshman year of high school. She was a precocious eighth-grader. She loved lots of excitement. One time she said she had to be home early. I came back to her house an hour later and she was out with the second shift. Another time, a guy she was going with at the same time I went with her picked me up downtown and took me over to the park and beat me up.

But she was the first and last girl in that little town I dared go out with. And I remember feeling that her parents really disapproved of me. I imagine what they really were feeling bad about wasn't me, but their hell-raising daughter.

Whatever the case, from then on I didn't even dare ask girls in our town for a date but went with girls from neighboring towns. I can see now that some of the local girls I liked were hoping I would ask them out and were even encouraging me as much as they could. But I couldn't see that at the time.

We lived on the wrong side of the tracks, too. How kids can figure out things like that is beyond me, but they see these distinctions and they are important. Those same distinctions were reflected in our little weekly newspaper's accounts of who had coffee with whom. I often felt you could put the hundred or so families in town on a list according to their social status with the list starting at the number one family, the Lunds, on down to the bottom family. And you could do it with no more than an analysis of who visited whom and just rule out the visits among relatives because they don't count.

When I was sixteen, my dad moved to Minneapolis to work in a war plant. He was investigated closely because he was in the security branch at the plant. The investigating agency wrote the theater owner in town investigating the suspicion my dad had stolen some equipment from an old deserted elevator. He may have picked up a few odds and ends that were going to waste, but he wouldn't have stolen anything big. Anyway, the theater owner wrote a letter on the incident saying that he thought there was more smoke than fire, and he sent a copy to our house with a note written on it, "I did the best for you I could, Tommy." I stumbled across a copy of the letter and I can still feel in my stomach the anger, shame, and humiliation of seeing that letter. It was very egotistical, I know. I wasn't worried about him but about what someone would think of me.

The incident also reminded me of an earlier one when I

was about five years old. I remember my dad and his many friends going out to his workshop and drinking alcohol poured out of large plain gallon cans and mixed with some sugar and water. One day he came home just wild. One of the local men he thought was his friend had turned him in for bootlegging. I don't know what happened because of it but I still remember that scene in the living room of that little house and my feelings.

After my dad was established in his defense plant job, we moved to the city. It was in the middle of my junior year. It was hard to leave then, but I would have had to leave someday anyway. And I'm afraid that no matter when I left, I would have been in the same kind of trouble.

From the time I left that small town I was running. I was caught up in a pattern of what Karen Horney called "overdriven strivings" and a frantic search for friends. Unfortunately the striving for accomplishment at any cost conflicted with the striving for friends.

When I was faced with a conflict between my strivings for recognition and my friends, I always sacrificed my friends. Also, I was so preoccupied with my business concerns that I couldn't really see my friends and their needs. In my family, it often took a drastic problem even to get my attention.

So it was this pattern I lived during high school in Minneapolis, college at the University of Minnesota, the advertising business in Kansas City, Minneapolis, and Chicago, and my own business.

Because I felt so second-rate I couldn't begin to use the potential I had.

If any of you think you may have been affected by similar childhood traumas, take a look at your life today. How much of what you are doing do you really believe in for you? And how much of what you are doing is to make an impression on someone else? That's a tough question to ask, let alone begin to answer. But it is crucial to us.

Why should we live out our lives in some vain attempt to please some nebulous, nameless "others"? Each of us is a child of God and an inheritor of the Kingdom of Heaven. Nothing second-rate about that. And our whole purpose in life is to move closer to what we are so we can do more naturally and easily the great things that are potentially in us whether that be President or a happy garbage collector. Either work is noble if we come to it out of love for the work.

When I started my own advertising agency at thirty-one I let the fact I felt second-rate rule me again. I had spent a year in Chicago as a copywriter at Leo Burnett. At that time, Burnett was one of the two or three hottest agencies in the country. They were doing the big cake ads for Pillsbury, smoothing out the Green Giant and establishing the Marlboro man. I wrote advertising for the Campbell Soup institutional campaign and Crane plumbing. I wasn't the best writer there but I wasn't the worst either.

But when I came back to Minneapolis to start my own business I didn't have the courage to go after big accounts. I only went after one good account and that was because the president of the company made me feel so welcome one time. Logically I knew what I was doing was wrong. But I couldn't handle those feelings of being second-rate. And that was pretty much the story of my life from the time I was young until I had my heart attack at thirty-six.

I was so concerned with my overdriven strivings that I didn't have time or energy for much else. In any conflict between my family and my business, my family almost always came second.

I remember reading a story recently about executive mobility. A young guy was going to be transferred for just one year and then transferred again. His wife had quickly reached the job she had dreamed of as an editor for a big newspaper's picture magazine.

They considered the alternatives, including divorce. But the only alternative they didn't consider was his getting a job with a different company or refusing the transfer so his wife could stay with her rare opportunity.

He reacted the way I did. I didn't consider my wife and family's needs. Now we try to work differently. We try to run our family on a basis of considering each person's need. When my wife felt she couldn't bear it on the farm, we moved to town. When I felt my bones would be more comfortable here in Montana, my wife gave up her beloved Minneapolis. No one in our family can always get exactly what he wants. But I think each of us feels that our needs will be considered and when our needs are of overriding importance they will rule.

My wife and I did all our vacationing with the family for many years. Now we take some vacations without the kids. When our vacation comes in the spring, we will go if there's no problem in the family preventing it. If there is a problem, we will go some other time.

It really hurts a family when it is run as a dictatorship, no matter who is the dictator, whether husband, wife, kids, or the parents of the husband or wife. I know a little of the hurt of the women in Women's Lib because I feel that I have often been dictated to and treated as a thing. They feel, for example, that they have been treated as sex objects. I know they have. I can remember a girl or two I dated just because she was so beautiful I could make the other guys jealous. I have been in situations where I felt I was a business object instead of a person with feelings. I felt I wasn't given any more consideration than a typewriter. So I support women's feelings without any reservations. Their feelings tell me they have been hurt bad and I believe them. I hope all women, and all men, and all children can find more dignity as persons—the dignity they are entitled to as God's children.

This is what we are trying to do in our family and what I am trying to do with the people around me. I know that

in our family we don't achieve our ideal of giving everyone equal rights, but we are working on it. Outside the
family, I know I don't do very well. In working with my
students I find I'm prejudiced against those who feel
grades are all-important. I'm struggling to overcome that
prejudice, but so far, I'm not doing too well. So back to
my earlier days.

I remember when I joined the Catholic Church, I was
twenty-six and was just starting in the advertising agency
business as a trainee. I was going at the business in my
usual, fanatical way. When I joined the Church I had the
flush of enthusiasm I bring to almost anything I try. But if
it doesn't pay off in externals, I drop it. I remember
thinking one day in church, "What kind of a Catholic
would I be if I approached my religion with the same intense energy and concentration I brought to the advertising business?" So I had a rare insight into the lack of balance in my life. That memory had a lasting effect on me
because I see now its influence when I had my heart attack. When I said, "From now on I'm not going to do
anything I don't believe in," I had to find out what I *did*
believe in.

I know how difficult it is for us to realize that here we
are at twenty, thirty, fifty, or even eighty and we still
might not know what we believe in. The idea seems so
strange and hard to accept. But I found out this was the
problem I had.

It took me five years, from age thirty-five to age forty,
before I had a very clear idea of what I believed in. In the
past six years, from forty to forty-six, I have gotten an
even clearer idea. So I found something that sounded very
simple was very hard to do.

I found, also, that I started out asking myself what the
deep me inside believed in. I have come to feel that God
is there, too. So now I have come to believe in a very
personal God who listens and speaks in my life, so I frequently during the day say, "Hey, God, what should I do

now?" And that question usually gives me a feeling for what to do. And it usually keeps me out of the sick games I have played so much—and still find myself playing sometimes.

So now I have a different feeling about my religion than I had when I first joined the church. I used to think I had to be more pious and holy. Today I'm saying "Hey, God, what should I do?" and then trying to do that as well as I can.

In all that screwed-up time before my heart attack there were two good periods that could have given me the clues to a better way of living. But I wasn't smart enough then to see them.

The first period was when I graduated from high school and went right into the Army. Two hundred of us from the Midwest enlisted for an Air Force college training unit in Cedar Rapids, Iowa because we were only seventeen and too young for active duty. We were grouped according to academic achievement and I was in the top group of forty, or Section I. We studied, played, and lived together as a unit. The security and the discipline did good things for me. I studied enough to get all A's but I had plenty of time left to have fun. I was dating two or three girls, wrote and produced an Army show, and fell madly in love with an older girl of nineteen.

My fellow students came to me for help with their math and physics and by teaching them I overlearned the subjects myself, which made the good grades easier to get. And I was studying because of my love of the subjects instead of to beat someone else. At that time calculus and physics were things of beauty and elegance to me.

Because of my good grades I didn't have to come back to the barracks until late Sunday evening. But sometimes I came home early just for the fun of it. It wasn't for lack of a social life, because I had plenty of that. And because I wasn't competing so viciously with the people around me, I had some good friends.

After nine months of this life, we were sent to basic training and then kicked out of the Air Force cadet program because it was 1945 and they didn't need any more trainees. So I was put in the regular Air Force and learned teletyping. But the vast impersonalness of the Air Force was more than I could take and the six months before I was given an early discharge were just a big, empty blank filled with boredom.

I found that when I lived in a structural situation that was small and well-suited to me I did great. But those good structured situations are very hard to find. Most of the time, I think, you have to build them for yourself. But the situations that you and I find good can give us precious clues as to the kind of situations we need and should find or build for ourselves.

The minute I went into the vast, impersonal structure of the Air Force, my adjustment came unglued, and it was even worse at the university.

When I came to the University of Minnesota with those good grades, Phi Beta Kappa was interested in me. But I couldn't stand the impersonalness again and my grades started down until I was just doing passing work when I graduated. I never heard from the honor fraternities again. I would have liked to join a social fraternity but I didn't have the courage to go through rushing. In my senior year I was asked to join one but by then I figured I would continue in my barbarian ways.

Here's an example of how poorly I did in school. I had Saul Bellow as an advanced composition teacher and didn't go to class. He was a fine teacher but I was so messed up nothing got through to me. I skipped about half my classes. I was busy being in all the student organizations on campus because I needed any kind of recognition and companionship so desperately.

I missed so many classes that for fifteen years I had nightmares in which I didn't even know what classes I was supposed to be in or where they were meeting. So I can see that in college I was acting in a way that deeply troubled another part of me.

And the sadness was that I got nothing but bad experiences from those years. I think I destroyed one college organization and may have crippled a couple of others through the selfishness and stupidity of my leadership.

The only good thing that happened in those years was meeting my wife. I was chaperon on a Snow Train to Duluth, met her, and started going with her immediately. I didn't think she was "intellectual" as most of my friends were. They were very busy solving the world's problems and ignoring their own. I held it against Jackie, a little, that she couldn't operate in those circles. Thank God she wasn't put off by it, and we got married a year after I graduated.

My oldest daughter was born sixteen months after we got married. She had a growth at the base of her brain that had to be removed when she was ten days old. She had some brain damage from spinal fluid pressure and she lost some brain to the surgery. We were so young and inexperienced and so little was known about her cerebral palsy then that we spent many years of agony with her. Now things have worked out far better than we could ever have hoped, but through the years that trial was living hell for Janet, my wife and I, and Janet's sister and three brothers, who came along over the next ten years.

I had come out of college so arrogant I thought I could run the world. When Janet was born, some of the awful false pride I had built up was destroyed. I was forced to realize I didn't run everything. I couldn't completely control my life as I had been inclined to think I could. So it was a hard, bitter lesson. It was as though God had my face down in the dirt with his foot on the back of my head. He was telling me to say "Nuff," while all the girls on the playground were watching my humiliation. There was no way out for me. I had to say "Nuff."

Besides the Air Force college days at Cedar Rapids,

the other good period when I was in some kind of harmony with life was after I switched from being an account executive to a copywriter at Bruce Brewer Advertising Agency in Minneapolis. I was a miserable failure as an executive. As a copywriter I found things went well, especially when Phil Burton came from Syracuse University for a year as my immediate superior. During that year I did outstanding work but soon I managed to foul things up again.

This was my coronary pattern in those early years. I spent my life floundering around in water over my head. As soon as I got so I could handle a situation, I found the calm and peace too hard to handle. I might be forced to take a look at myself. So I would run out and stir up some new hell for myself by entering deeper water than I could handle.

Leo Burnett, whose work I had studied and admired, was in town making a speech. So I wrote out my advertising creed and handed it to him after his speech. I didn't keep a copy but I had written things like: "Remember that you're always writing advertising to your brother and you don't lie to your brother." And, "Remember that your reader is a twenty-four-year-old girl whose mother is dying of cancer and write to her accordingly."

Burnett asked me to come down to Chicago for an interview and I was hired. My wife was smart enough to see that it was wrong to move away from my present success but I wouldn't listen to her and we moved anyway. After three months I saw my mistake and told her I would stick it out a year and then we would go back to Minneapolis.

Near the end of that year I went to Minneapolis and found a job with a big agency and gave thirty days notice at Leo Burnett. The next week the guy who hired me called and told me he had changed his mind. I couldn't believe it. I was in deep trouble. I bundled up the family and we took the night train to Minneapolis. I felt so poor that I wouldn't even rent any 25¢ pillows so the family could sleep better.

When we got to Minneapolis Jackie took the kids to her folks' place and I went to a phone booth to start calling. I had to get a copywriting job in thirty days or start my own business, so I started working on both problems at once. It was Thursday morning. By Friday evening I had four small clients lined up, which would be halfway to a bare break-even in my own business. I could see I couldn't get a full-time copy job in thirty days. So I was in business for myself—something I had always wanted but something I now see was very bad for me because there were no people working with me and no good structure to help me. At the time, I wasn't capable of seeing my needs.

We found a house and moved September 1, 1957. Our fourth child, Joe, was born the end of October. Through frantic work, I lined up enough business the first month to break even. For the first two or three years business was good. But again I managed to screw things up. I started spending more money than we had so I was constantly under intense pressure, which was partly why I spent: I needed the pressure to keep me from seeing what I was doing to myself.

And I also needed to spend money to show people how great I was. I hadn't been in business more than a year when we went house hunting. At that time, the big, old mansions were selling for $25,000 to $35,000. They were huge, imposing houses. They were a little more than I could afford at that time, but I wanted one anyway. I remember thinking as we drove down one long, shady street of old mansions how impressed my uncle Virgil would be to come visit me on that block. I was still living with ghosts and listening to them instead of myself.

We bought a house we could afford and I set out to garden. I found a lady who had the most beautiful garden in Minneapolis and started trying to equal her. I worked madly at that garden. It was a great way to relax.

I soon saw that I could never impress anyone with that house so I started hunting for a fancy one. I found a nice new colonial in a high-powered suburb. Jackie didn't want us to move but she couldn't help enjoying the beautiful house. I fouled things up there by spending lots of money again. If I had gone slow and easy there would have been no problem but I went out and bought all new furniture (for downstairs where it showed, to hell with the bedrooms). We had a little sports car for Jackie to drive but the engine went so we bought her a new one for Christmas. With all those self-created pressures building up, my heart attack wasn't too far away. I'm sure that with what I was doing to myself, something had to give. If it hadn't been my heart, it would have been my stomach, liver, or maybe even my mind that went.

The summer before, I had started to see trouble coming and made a faint attempt to get out. I thought of going back to school and getting a master's degree in physics, which I had loved so much. Alfred Nier was willing to be my adviser. He thought that even with my master's, I would end up communicating physics instead of working physics problems. What a wise man. I went to work that summer trying to renew my math, but I had been away from it too long to bring back the speed and accuracy I used to have. I was planning to milk my advertising business by giving it minimum attention and go to school, too. So I still wasn't willing to surrender. I had to control things, and for me, I was satisfied with only the tightest kind of control.

All that time trouble was building up. And my deeper self wanted out. It was just a question of finding the way out. The trouble with heart attacks as a way out is that they can be fatal. But heart attacks also give you a nice excuse to stop fighting so hard. So heart attack it was.

4

Jackie

How can I write of my husband's life before I knew him? I cannot with accuracy. I can only tell about impressions that I received, after the fact.

Jess was big, handsome—a bald Paul Newman. Blue eyes that were huge and long-lashed. Roman nose. A big mouth that could split his face with a grin or pout like a two-year-old. He was a senior at the University of Minnesota and I was a seventeen-year-old freshman. He had been in the Army Air Force toward the end of World War II and fought the battle of St. Louis on frequent passes from Scott Field, Illinois. He was a "stud" to me (to borrow a very apt phrase from my teenagers).

A loner. Jess belonged to a lot of organizations at the university. He was even president of a few. But always he felt away from his fellow students. He always seemed to be waiting to get slapped down. I couldn't understand why he was that way. To me he was so superior. I puzzled over it.

Another thing bothered me in these early years of our

dating and marriage. When I felt unsure or inferior, I took my marbles and went home. I reacted to difficulty by retreating. Not Jess. The more shaky he was, the more he took on. He swallowed challenge in huge gulps. He didn't even stop to chew. If he choked on a challenge he spit it out and greedily bit off another hunk, bigger and tougher than before. I became exhausted just watching him. He never could be still. Not even for a minute. Even relaxation was exhausting.

When I relax, I collapse. I read a book. I sit and count the dust balls rolling around on the floor. I watch TV.

When Jess relaxed he got up at 5 A.M. and tramped through the woods until night fell, carrying a twenty-five-pound gun on his shoulder and looking for grouse or pheasant or even a luckless squirrel. Or he went fishing.

The few times I fished, I took some worms and a pole and sat on a bank or in a boat and contemplated my navel.

Jess spent until midnight the night before sorting his tackle box, putting new line on his pole. Then he got up at 4 or 5 A.M. and rushed around getting together enough supplies for a safari. Then he drove—always too fast—to a lake that was always difficult to get to and then waded out to his armpits constantly, flailing his line up, down, whoops, his line was in a tree, out of the water. Unsnag the line. Into the water. Flail. Flail. Damn, that fish got away. It was a life-and-death expedition. Jess and the fish. Jess and the partridge. It was exhausting to watch.

He was hard on life and life was hard on him. Why? I don't know. What makes a man tick? All I know is that Jess has to gallop through life. And I trot behind panting, trying to keep up until I periodically collapse and say to hell with life and him and everything.

But Jess never did collapse. He just kept running. Running and running right into a heart attack.

Another memory comes to me. Air Corps days. A doctor put Jess in the hospital down in Wichita Falls, Texas. He was an eighteen-year-old recruit. The doctor felt there was something wrong with his heart. One of the chambers was enlarged. Jess sat in bed and made a tooled leather billfold. No other doctor could ever find anything wrong. They didn't discharge him for medical reasons. But was it a clue?

Jess's family—wonderful people. Farmers, ranchers, smalltown people. They were a clan in the true sense of the word. But they were competitive one with another. At the top of the clan sat Grandpa. Jess Plummer Lair. Bigger, stronger, more silent than any of his sons.

Fluttering around Grandpa was Grandma, Janet Mary Robertson Lair. She was like a little wren when I knew her. She only had a few years left to live. Bad heart.

There was Tommy, Jess's father. A loud, laughing, boisterous charmer. Short, stocky, massive chest and shoulders. He lived life in extremes, happy and loud one minute, madder than hell and loud the next. Generous to a fault: buy the luxuries, let the necessities take care of themselves. He was to die in his early fifties. Bad heart.

Bertha Eggen Lair. I didn't know how to take Bertha in those first years. She was a silent, non-reacting Norwegian. She could cook better than anyone I knew. She was shy and quiet in contrast to her hurricane of a husband. Her family were all Montanans. Tommy met Bertha in Absarokee, Montana, when he went to work for Uncle Tom Robertson there. They were married in Billings. I never knew Bertha's parents, for they had both died in the 1930s. One of them with a bad heart, maybe both, I'm not sure.

Pride. I guess pride is the word that best sums up the Lair clan. They were proud, hard-working people. They wanted a better life for their children. They held their heads high. They were white, Anglo-Saxon, Protestant. So what was this Catholic girl with a medal around her neck doing with one of their own? Unthinkable!

By going with me, Jess did it again. He was always doing something a little different from the rest. When Jess turned Catholic, more than one of the relatives felt relieved that Tommy hadn't known about it before he died. Looking back, I think Tommy would have taken it more in stride than some of the aunts did. And I know Bertha never said an unkind word in our presence about it.

Grandma Bert, as the children call her, how I have come to love that woman. She is a rock, one who accepts all that fate has dealt her without a stir of self-pity. As the years have gone by she has become lovelier. Age deals gracefully with the stouthearted. She is Ruth of the Bible. "Whither thou goest, I will go. Thy people shall be my people." Those two sentences were written about my mother-in-law. I know her. She'll read this and not say a word. Maybe a frown or a little grimace, or a small giggle. Those Norwegians don't have to much to say of a personal nature.

When I married Jess, my mother said, "It will be good to get a little Norwegian in the family to cool down the Irish, Scottish, French, German blood." I think the reverse is true also. It's good for Jess to have a wife and children around with some ability to express their feelings.

Now, I grant that tears and laughter come in superabundance to us hotbloods. But we do know a feeling when we see one. We are not stoics. Manure is manure and a rose is a rose and by God we not only know the difference, we'll tell you about it—instantly. That is one of the basic differences between my husband and myself. He lives by denial. As long as it isn't mentioned, it doesn't exist. Not me. If you can't recognize horse manure when you see it, and get it out from under your nose fast—you're in trouble. This is my biggest contribution to Jess. It's meant a lot to our marriage.

Jess is a perfectionist also. That's wonderful. But, like any quality, if you carry it to extremes it gets pretty messy.

A story from Jess's childhood illustrates how early he

was a persnickety person: When Jess was in third grade, he had a long walk home from school. One day, he received a message from his bowels that they needed relief —now. He relieved himself. In his pants. When he arrived home, Bertha asked, "Why didn't you go in the cornfield?"

"I didn't want to get the corn dirty."

Now that's perfectionism. Mess yourself up but don't upset the pristine grandeur of the cornfield.

God bless him—that's my husband. And he still is doing the equivalent to himself today.

I have read many books on the heart in the past ten years. The term "coronary personality" has become a household word. I'd like to share my feelings about such a personality; see if you recognize anyone in my description.

I feel that an awful lot of the charmers of this world are coronary personalities. They are people who are always bouncy and energetic. People who are happy to see you, people who are in many cases the life of the party.

Many times I have felt that my coronary husband had a circuit broken in his system. This circuit is the one that tells us when to quit. My husband never knew when he was tired. He worked at a trot or gallop all day long although oftentimes he accomplished little. When he was at his worst he caused tremendous commotion, a lot of anxiety, but rarely finished or even started some very crucial things that needed doing.

I have noticed too in many people of this type that their emotions are often very raw and close to the surface. They seem to get teary very easily.

Now that I am older, I have come to believe that men *are* a lot more emotional than women, but still it seems to me that my coronary darling does feel things more deeply than most.

A red flag that I have learned to recognize through the years is depression. When Jess is depressed I look for heart trouble. It follows many times as night follows day.

Depression is a fooler, though. Jess has what can only be called "agitated depression." It doesn't, to this layman, resemble depression.

I think of extreme depression as the kind that just knocks us out. We don't want to do anything, we cry and mope a lot.

Not Jess. As he becomes depressed he begins winding up like a top. He becomes quite a good deal more active, and works himself up until he is frenzied. He responds to feelings of depression with work, work, work.

The doctor's tendency in this situation is to give Jess tranquilizers. These only make him worse. We stay away from medication of this sort as much as possible.

From frenzy Jess works up to heart trouble. His frenzied activity even shows in his "play." If it's wintertime, he skis harder than anyone else. If it's spring or summer, his horses get worked to death, and he fishes overmuch. If it's fall, he hunts to extreme.

Extremes. I guess this is the word we all recognize as applying to coronary personalities. If they smoke, it's two to four packs a day. If they are gastronomes, they eat like Henry VIII.

If their hang-up is business, they put in eighteen hours a day.

If they like to party, they are the first to arrive and the last to leave. And they usually can consume a lot more food and liquor than anyone else there.

They live hard. And many times I fear they are, or seem to be, very angry people.

Jess does not have a mean bone in his body. He is the most patient of men. And yet—Jess, forgive me—I often feel that he is seething with an unnamed anger at persons or things that he does not even know about.

I wonder if men have had untold damage done to them by being taught to control their emotions. Living has taught me that men like to believe they are more objective

than women but rarely are. That men like to believe they
are stronger than women but rarely are. That men like to
believe they can roll with the punches but rarely can. I
believe the burying of their emotions makes them much
more vulnerable than women.

I see these traits in all kinds of men, from all walks of
life. Up-tight doctors who hurry and scurry, bemoaning
their work load, yet unable to stop themselves. Up-tight
ranchers bemoaning the work it takes to make a dollar
these days, yet unwilling to make adjustments. An owner
of a service station, exhausted because he won't work just
an eight-hour shift. He has to control every open minute
of his gas station.

And underneath all of this hurry and scurry I see
frightened little boys who find the world a hard and
frightening place. Who feel that they must control every
facet of life lest they be crushed.

How very sad. And how much they need to know that
they can "let go" and that God is in His Heaven, and we
wives who depend on them can stand beside them and
help, instead of behind them pushing, or leaning.

I am no judge of how early rearing places these strains
on men. I do not pretend to have any answers for you,
but I do feel that Jess came to me at age twenty-three
with a pretty well-set psyche. And it is my job to help the
good part of that psyche grow and encourage the bad part
of it to wither and die. I do believe that I can make some
difference.

5

Jess

Moving to the farm outside Minneapolis was the only positive thing I had done so far in all my life other than marry my wife. I had wandered into the two previous good periods in my life instead of seeking them out. In the case of the farm, my wife and I went out and did the thing we both believed in. And because we were doing what we believed in we took our first faltering step down the long road that leads to a happier, more fruitful life.

My wife wanted to move to the farm because I needed it, we could live cheaply, and our family could be close together. It still must have been very hard for Jackie to move. She has never talked about it much but she was leaving her dream house and a way of life to which she was accustomed to go in search of my dream. I had been raised on a farm. I left while I was still young so I was short on the technical information like what to feed chickens, but my bones felt comfortable on the farm.

When I was in a fancy place, I was always conscious of what I was doing. Was I using the right fork? Was I doing the right thing? Everything in life as a businessman was an effort because there was nothing in the way I was brought up to prepare me for any of my experiences. Until I was eighteen years old I had never eaten a meal in a house where there were two forks at all the evening meals. I don't think I was in a businessman's office ten times before I was twenty-one. So the life of a businessman and fancy homes were very foreign and frightening to me. Everything I did had to be thought out and done consciously.

I'm sure most of my trouble reflected my own insecurity. But I remember reading a study on top executives in *Fortune* one time. Most presidents of companies were sons of white-collar workers or managers. One of the study's conclusions was that it was almost impossible for an executive to jump up two steps on the social ladder without having emotional problems. This was why so many blue-collar workers' sons ended up in middle management where the social demands weren't so high. Then, the next generation, their sons, could be company presidents.

So on the farm I was back in my element. I felt at home in barns and open country. And Jackie, as she had done so often before, rose to the occasion. She took an old farmhouse and with white paint and pretty curtains and tablecloths made a beautifully warm home. It was so pleasant-looking most people reacted visibly to it.

Our friends came to visit and enjoyed themselves. And my mind, for the first time, was clear enough so I could enjoy them. Because I was more open to life, the people who are always at our elbows waiting to love us and nurture us could begin to teach me about life.

Bud was an old bachelor who had thirty or forty horses. We wanted to buy a couple of horses, so my neighbor suggested we see Bud. We found he wanted an outrageous price, $250, for a horse worth half that. He loved his horses so much and was so interested in their marital affairs that he could not bear to be parted from them even though his pastures were bare. He lived in a wreck of a house with a cleared space large enough for a bed and an oven to heat up his TV dinners.

As I was talking to Bud about his horses he happened to mention that he had rented one to someone. I asked him if he would rent one to us if we would let him breed the horse so he could have a colt. He thought that was a good idea and rented us a horse with a colt at her side, and the rent was low even with the use of a saddle and bridle thrown in.

We enjoyed the horse and colt so much we went back and rented another horse so two of us could ride. Bud would stop by to check his horses and see how they were getting along. Jackie was baking homemade bread in those days. Bud must have had a nose like a pointer dog because he always seemed to show up just as the bread came out of the oven. He would sit around and visit, and because Jackie had seen what he called home, she would make him stay for supper.

Bud loved to visit, talk about horses, and tell stories. He was a sharp contrast to the people I had spent my time with up to that point—people to whom money was so important. For Bud, money was on the bottom of his list of priorities. There had been people like that in Bricelyn, Minnesota. There were people like that in Minneapolis, too, but I managed not to meet them. In a small town, I couldn't avoid all sides of life and Bud was a side I needed to be reminded of badly. And thanks to him, Jackie and I could sit in the shade in front of the house in lawn chairs and watch the two horses and the colt play in the pasture in front of the house.

So often people tell me that they can't live the kind of life they want to. I think our experiences on the farm are a good example of how you can do that. If you want the same experience we had on the farm in a high-quality way with thoroughbred horses, colonial houses, white board fences, and stylish neighbors, it costs so much money that you almost have to inherit it or kill yourself paying for it. But we were enjoying what to us were the essentials of that experience in a set of farm buildings we rented for $60 a month and two horses we rented for $100 a year.

One of the sad things was that we were living what the man who owned the place was just dreaming of. Our landlord was a salesman who had bought the farm with the idea of building a big new house there, putting up white board fences, and filling the pastures with white-faced cattle. The sadness was that he was so busy making money to pay for all those things sometime ahead in the future that he couldn't enjoy them now. Because we weren't quite so fussy about things like white board fences, we were living his dream.

When I watched that tired, driven man come to his farm and be so torn between the run-down way the farm actually was and the way he wanted it to be I saw how big a price we can pay when our life is too tied up in dreams.

There was a big contrast in life just across the road from me. Bits Osterbauer was about thirty-one when I first met him. He had the wisdom only a few get when they are one hundred and one. Bits was renting the pasture on our farm for his cattle, so he would come over often. He was always ready with help when it was needed and in the beginning I needed plenty of help.

I began to see that as a neighbor I was getting behind so I looked around for things I could do for him and found some. At one time it got to the point where I think Bits felt I was even a little ahead of him in the helping-each-other department because I noticed him doing a bunch of things for us all of a sudden. I found myself thinking, "What are you doing, Bits, keeping score?" And the answer I saw was "Yes." Because we do keep score.

Bits was wise enough to see the bad feeling that can come when one man feels too much in another man's debt. All this went on without our saying a word about our feelings to each other. With Bits, you didn't need to. He knew how you felt and you knew that he knew without talking about it. We talked about other things. The feelings were expressed in between the lines.

We had a chicken house and Jackie wanted some laying hens so I asked Bits to pick out twelve layers for us. I knew enough about chickens to know they all didn't lay every day. But the morning after he delivered them, when I found eleven eggs from the twelve hens, I jumped in my car and raced over to Bits's place to give him hell for selling me a bad hen. He really laughed.

I began to be quite active when we were on the farm. I rode horseback a lot with Jackie, my son Jess, Jr., or my daughter Barbara. We had a game preserve right back of our place with some trails through the oaks and maples, so the country was all reds, yellows, and golds in the fall. Jess, Jr., and I would come back from riding and race across the pasture to the barn yelling like Indians. On the farm, for the first time, I was able to be a real part of the family. There were a couple of good fishing holes in the game preserve. My three boys and I would go fishing there. It was fun for all of us because we could sit on the bank and catch bullheads and sunfish as fast as we could bait our hooks. One day my son, Joe, who was just five, came home and told his mother: "I caught ten bullheads and one fish that was full of sun!"

And I went back to school. My first tentative plan was to teach. I found I could get a master's degree and teach in college in only one year, whereas it would take me two years to prepare myself as a high school teacher. Also, I thought I could teach big kids better than little ones. So I went back to the university to get a master's degree in journalism with the idea of teaching advertising in some college community.

When I applied to graduate school I was nearly rejected. My grades were poor but I had taken a couple of aptitude tests fifteen years before and on the basis of those tests they let me in on probation. The lady who admitted me called my undergraduate record "undistinguished," which, of course, it was.

So I took courses in journalism with a statistics minor. Some of the journalism courses I had to take were in advertising and they were taught by a young Ph.D. who had worked in advertising research a couple of summers. I think all my experience in advertising may have scared him a little but I kept my mouth shut and got good grades so I could show them I was a real scholar and get off probation.

I had graduated from the university with a major in journalism in 1948, and one of my favorite professors was still there, Fred Kildow. Fred had had a distinguished career as a professor but he didn't have a doctorate. He stopped me one day and told me that if I wanted to go into college teaching I needed a doctorate. My practical experience in advertising wouldn't count for much. Without the doctorate, my academic higher-ups would be looking down my tonsils and calling me a second-class citizen. They would do with me as they had with him, using the lack of a doctorate to disparage his accomplishments.

By that time I could see that I didn't want to teach advertising. I had had some bad experiences in advertising and there was no way I could encourage other people to go into it or stay there. One old art director friend's comment came back to me. Wes Marquette had said to me: "Look around you, Jess, and see how many gray-haired art directors there are in advertising agencies." There were hardly any. Most of them got out and went into other fields of art direction because the advertising agency business is a killer unless you're made of steel and don't mind the sight of blood.

We had been to Montana on vacations when I was a kid and I thought I would like to go there and live. So I modified my goal in light of my new experiences and decided to get a Ph.D. and try teaching in a Montana college.

I couldn't have made that decision if school hadn't been easy for me. It wasn't because I was all that smart. I was worried how I would do before I started. But one kind lady at Allison-Williams in Minneapolis told me she had gone back and it was easy for her and most of the other older students.

When I got to college I found out why. My fellow students were much smarter than I. Some of them had IQs twice my weight. But they couldn't concentrate. When they were studying their heads were full of questions like, "Who am I, what am I, where am I?" When I sat studying I knew who I was: "I am Jess Lair, I am sitting at home studying and the quicker I get this stuff learned, the quicker I can stop studying and be with my family."

So all through graduate school I was able to get my studying done quickly and still have time for my wife, my children, and myself.

I was faced with the problem of what field to get a Ph.D. in. I went through a copy of the graduate bulletin and looked up a number of majors I was interested in: anthropology, American studies, journalism, sociology, and psychology. I checked the courses in each of them. There were more courses in psychology that I thought I would like to take so I chose that as my major.

Fortunately, I had a friend in that field, too. Whit Longstaff had taught me a course in the psychology of advertising in 1947. I had returned to see him occasionally. I went to him and asked him if he would be my Ph.D. adviser and help me get a degree. He said he would be happy to. Right then, he did a very helpful thing for me. He went to his files and pulled out a Ph.D. dissertation. He said, "You see this? It was written by one of my students who is just now starting his course work. But this is a good dissertation and it's already written. I think you can write yours while you do your course work so you can get through faster."

Bless that man for his faith in me and his counsel. I took this advice and because of it I was able to finish my Ph.D. in two years.

So after just nine months on the farm I had finished my course work on the master's and was ready to start my Ph.D. and everything was going as smooth as silk. I was still wrestling with the aftereffects of old problems but I wasn't making new ones for myself and I wasn't getting in my own way and fighting myself. My bones were comfortable and I was finally able to start listening to the people around me. They were telling me the same things my wife had been trying to tell me for fourteen years but I was finally ready to listen. Life is a beautiful teacher and if you don't pay attention to her little blows, you'll soon get a bigger blow. In my case, it took a heart attack to get my attention.

One of my other teachers on the farm was Phil Gatzow. Phil believed in subsistence living. By living modestly, Phil was able to retain his independence and dignity and live right where he wanted to. He was such a good trapper that he made enough in the fall trapping plus some work at the gas station so most of the time he was free.

Bits told me there was a trout stream nearby and that Phil knew where it was. I stopped at the gas station in Forest Lake and introduced myself as Bits's friend. I had a glimmer of intuition that told me to curb my hard-charging self a little and go as softly as I could. Phil is a quiet, slowgoing person and he brings this out in the people he is with, too, so he deserves part of the credit.

But anyway, I let him know I was interested in trout fishing and if he was willing, would like to learn something from him about it. I was lucky and he agreed to take me with him.

A few days later he picked me up and we went ten

miles north of our farm to a small spring-fed stream through the marsh that ran clear all year long. Phil showed me exactly how to rig my hook, how to put the worm on, and how to present it to the trout. He walked along fishing and coaching me. He caught ten nice brook trout while I caught two. But with practice I eventually got the knack of it.

One of the first times we went fishing, we stopped at a small bridge over a stream. We got out of the car and looked things over. Phil said, "A family has been here fishing, but it is no problem, they weren't after trout."

I was puzzled. "How do you know all that?" I couldn't see anything.

He showed me the tracks of a man, a woman wearing shoes with small heels, and a child. He showed me the circle where a pail had sat and the little globs of gravel from the condensation running down the side. So it was probably a minnow bucket, and small brook trout aren't usually fished for with minnows. The whole story was there for me to see. All I had to do was look and think.

Another time we were walking through the woods in early fall. Phil said, "Looks like five deer went through here recently. They could be just ahead of us." By now I knew Phil well enough to know he loved playing the "old trapper" role. But I thought he was carrying things a little too far.

"Phil, how can you say that?"

"Look, Jess, see over there in the grass beneath the oaks, you can see the grass is bent a different way so it doesn't shine like the undisturbed grass does." I looked and I could see what he meant.

"Okay, Phil, I see that. But why five deer?"

"Look further and you'll see where they split up and there are five separate tracks."

Sure enough. I looked carefully and I could dimly see

the five tracks that split apart and then mixed in together again.

I've never forgotten that experience. It has helped me in life and in psychology. There are so many things around us to be seen. They don't force themselves on our attention but they are there waiting for us to observe. But again, as Phil taught me, we have to be going along slowly and unhurriedly with our minds clear or we can't see anything.

Using this idea, I have come to be much more sensitive to all the signs in my life and their significance to me. These are the things I used to ignore because in my introspection I had my head buried so deep in my own navel. Now I'm trying to pay attention to the priceless clues that are all around me to tell me what my real self is.

One sign was in my undergraduate grades. I looked at my transcript after I got into graduate school and saw that my worst grades were in advertising, my major, and my best grades were in the theoretical subjects like economics and psychology. But when I was twenty I didn't pay any attention or give any respect to those valuable clues. I try to now.

I find my students have a hard time with this idea of paying attention to the clues in their lives. They find it so hard to believe they should pay attention to what they like. They can't believe work can be easy and fun. They are convinced they can and should do hard, distasteful things and use their will power to force them to do them.

But here I am telling them to look at what's easy and fun in their lives as a basis for choosing a career, a wife, and a place to live.

Twenty years ago I found Reilly's book on *How to Make Your Living in Four Hours a Day.* That's an interesting title. But the rest of the title is more interesting. It is *Without Feeling Guilty About It,* and that's where the

Puritan in us comes in. If we don't feel bad about it, it can't be work.

Reilly calls work only those things he doesn't like to do. His writing and speaking he didn't count as work because he enjoyed doing them.

After twenty years of working on Reilly's idea, I can see his hope was that by using his idea and the clues in our life, we could make our living without "working at all."

I don't count this kind of writing as work. I enjoy doing it. I'm teaching half time now and most of the time I enjoy that, so I would do it even if I didn't need the money. But man, do I still have problems feeling guilty about it! It is so hard for me just to sit and relax and do nothing. So far I need to be skiing or fishing or hunting or working around the house or barn as my relaxation. Very little of my time is spent just doing next to nothing.

So look at your life and the clues that lie close to you that tell you what your work should be, where you should live, and what you should become. Those clues are all around you. The only problem is they are so close to you and you take them for granted so much that it is hard for you to appreciate how important they really are to you.

I don't know how much education my friend Phil Gatzow had, but he sure kept on learning all his life. As I mentioned, he had fashioned a subsistence level of living that let him live the way he wanted. Bits had done the same thing. They didn't live fancy. But they had a few things that were really important to them. And because they were free of all kinds of self-imposed money pressures, they were able to be strong, contributing people to their families and the people around them instead of being blind fools going through life hurting the people around them and not knowing how they hurt.

That reminds me of an incident that happened in about 1956 when I was with Bruce Brewer Advertising Agency. I was late for an appointment in St. Paul. I was rushing as usual. A deep, early spring snow was turning to slush. Up ahead on the sidewalk, an old man and a little boy were walking. Just as I came alongside, I hit a particularly deep puddle and spashed slush and water all over them. So that was my happy contribution to their lives that morning. In that case, I saw what I did. Even worse have been all the times when I've done something like this and not even noticed it.

It used to be that I was speeding all the time. I was rushing to make up time and driving with one eye on traffic and the other on my rear-view mirror to see if a cop was following me. I got my share of speeding tickets. I should have had lots more. I'm lucky I didn't kill someone.

Now I'm usually not rushing so I'm not speeding. I'm still way too absent-minded so I have trouble slowing down to fifteen miles an hour for school zones. The way I've solved that problem temporarily is I drive the long way around so I don't go near any schools. This protects the kids and me, too. But gradually I find I'm less and less distracted when I drive, which is just another reflection of getting time pressure out of my life.

About the time I was on the farm, I found a study on heart attacks that was done in San Francisco. Two groups of researchers working independently were asked to predict the likelihood of coronaries in the same group of businessmen. One group used the cholesterol level as their predictor and selected a subgroup as being high risks for having heart attacks.

The other group of researchers used a test to pick high-risk heart attack men. The test consisted of bringing the men in for interviews by appointment. The interviewer was purposefully quite late for the appointment. He went ahead with a routine list of questions, but the real test was to see how the businessmen reacted to the time pressure. Some men were infuriated with the psychologist for being late and they had difficulty handling their bad feelings during the interview. Other men accepted the delay well and were quickly able to get on with the routine interview.

The psychologists used their observations in the interview to divide the businessmen into two categories: Type A, those who fought the clock, and Type B, those who didn't. The prediction was that the Type A businessmen would be more likely to have heart attacks. In the next five years the time pressure test proved more accurate than the cholesterol test. This isn't to say cholesterol isn't important. But it says to me that fighting the clock is a more dangerous way to live. And, of course, we don't need to choose. We can learn to handle time with less pressure and watch our cholesterol too.

I read another piece of research at about the same time. Subjects were placed in a hospital and then were deliberately made angry. It was found their cholesterol level went up when they got angry. So it could be that the way we feel has a lot to do with many of the body chemistry changes we see in people. Whatever the case, I have seen enough of the problems caused by rushing through life and being blinded by my rushing that I don't want to live that way. Even if it doesn't prolong my life a single day, some moderation in my rushing can make the days I have far more enjoyable.

But I noticed that a lot of the advice to heart patients tells them to stop rushing without any sense of how hard it is. Unless we can get at some of our problems in our life and do something about them, we aren't going to stop our rushing.

As I was mentioning earlier, Phil and Bits had fashioned a subsistence living for themselves. The phrase "subsistence level" I just recently got from a book on the people Wyeth puts on canvas. While the genius of the paintings is his, some of the greatness comes from the people. The man who posed for "The Patriot" told of seeing the subsistence level farmers in France in World War I. When he returned home from the war he was determined to find a way to live off the land, and he made it.

So many people today, especially the young, are screaming out against materialism. And they are correct. But many blame society for doing this to them and fail to see that there are plenty of people in society who aren't materialists. And often I see these same young people denying their own materialism. The student parking lots are filled with fancy cars. A guy who thought of himself as a hippie had a stereo set, a pile of records, a big portrait camera, some antique furniture, two pair of Head skis, Lange boots, and a lever-action .30-30.

I have a picture in my office of the possessions Gandhi had when he was killed. He left behind two pair of sandals, a cloak, a pen, a watch, and a couple of bowls. Now there was a real anti-materialist.

I grant I'm a materialist. But I see some differences in my materialism before and after my heart attack. Most of the things I have now aren't fancy, they are just useful. And I use them often and hard. My cars are old and beat-up. My skis, ski boots, and saddles are secondhand. My horses aren't papered. To a degree, my possessions have come to be just tools and I don't have a big ego investment in them as I used to have. Before, I saw myself as being defined by my possessions. That was pretty sick.

As I attempt it, I am finding more and more how hard it is for me to settle down in one place and submit myself to the routine of just living. I still haven't come close. But I have an idea of what I'm trying to do and how difficult it is today. And I think a lot of frantic running around the country and buying things is an attempt to run away from the self rather than a search for the self.

I think the thing I need to see about my materialism is that it is mine. Sure there is a materialistic streak in our society. But there is also an anti-materialistic streak. And I had a choice as to which one of those two tendencies I responded to. I see now that I needed materialism so I could use my possessions to build myself up and put other people down. I don't see that I will be able to get rid of that materialism unless I see my problem very clearly and avoid blaming other people for my sick choices.

Also, if other people laid their materialism on me, then I'm a prisoner of them and there is no hope for me. But if I laid that materialism on myself, then I can take it off and there is hope for me. And I need hope.

I had some more teachers on the farm. Each fall three of Bits's cousins, Moats, Eddie, and LeRoy Osterbauer, came for deer hunting, the preparations before, and the deer butchering afterward. Some other relatives came, too. The first fall on the farm I didn't go hunting. But the second fall I had been in the woods following deer trails and Bits invited me to hunt. I could stand at the end of the drives so it wouldn't be too much exertion for me.

Early the first morning, I was one of a line of standers. The drivers were coming through the woods toward us. Bits had stationed me in the center of the line of standers. I can see now he did it so I would have the best chance. Sure enough, as the drivers got nearer, a deer materialized out of the marsh just in front of me and I got him. There was much celebrating because he almost got away. (I know some of your sensibilities may be offended by hunting, but it is something that is still important to me.)

The next morning I was standing watching a deer trail and another deer went by and I shot. But I only wounded the deer slightly. Bits and I trailed him a ways but Bits had to go to church. So he left and I kept on the trail. I went very slowly because I was still being extra careful about my heart. But Jackie didn't know that.

When I didn't come home by ten o'clock in the morning she got worried. When she saw Bits and found out I was alone she was frantic. She put on a red pajama top of mine so she would be wearing something red and headed into the woods in the direction Bits had pointed out. It was marshy and Jackie had no idea of where the trails were so she went right across country. By this time I had

given up on finding the deer because there was no more
blood in the trail. I was slowly walking out of the woods
and saw Jackie coming. She was just wild. She had lost
one shoe but her feet were so cold and numb she didn't
know it. If she had had the gun instead of me, I'm sure
she would have shot me—and with a certain amount of
justice.

That was how I started deer hunting. I have been big
game hunting each fall since and it has always been a terrible worry for Jackie. One year in Montana I gave up my
fruitless pursuit for elk one fall to make it easier on her.
But I was so unhappy sitting home that with my pouting I
made Jackie even more miserable than she was when I
was hunting. So we agreed that this evidently was one of
those things that I had to do and she would have to adjust
to it.

From Bits's cousins, and particularly Moats, I learned
how much fun people can have together. Moats loved to
play a poker game called "In Between." You get two
cards face up and then bet on whether you can get a card
in between the two cards. When I had a two and a king, I
would bet a dollar because any card from a three to a
queen would win and the odds were heavily in my favor.
But I learned from Moats that that's a dumb way to play
the game. Only someone who is greedy and doesn't understand life would play it my way.

Moats would bet a dollar when he had a two and a
four. Only a three-spot would win for him and there are
only four of them out of fifty-two. So his odds were thirteen to one against him and he was making an even
money bet. Financially what he was doing didn't make
sense. But it did to Moats. Because if he lost, it was funny
betting against such long odds and if he won, that was
even funnier. He would lose some money playing that
game but he made the party a happy one because of the
fun he brought to it.

One day we were standing at the edge of a patch of

trees. We had been hunting for two days so we were both tired. We were just standing at the end. Just then we heard a yell and a deer ran out the side. Moats and I both grabbed our guns and shot at the same instant. The deer dropped. Without a second for thought, Moats turned to me and said, "Hell, Jess, we got it. It won't make a good story at all." He's the only deer hunter I have ever seen who appreciates all the years of fun in telling the stories about the deer you missed and sees laughing at yourself as being more valuable than just shooting a deer. One year he turned around and saw a deer following him. He shot it and claimed it was self-defense. He won't admit it, but he is so afraid of the dark, he won't hunt until the sun is up.

So from these varied characters, my teachers of life, I learned some new lessons about what life is really like.

At about the same time, a fellow graduate student told me about B. F. Skinner's book *Analysis of Behavior*. It is a programmed textbook by Holland and Skinner. It needs no previous knowledge of psychology to read it. The student told me she learned as much psychology from that one book as she had from any three courses she had taken. I took her suggestion, bought the book, and started working through it. It was very valuable in showing me how to control my own behavior better.

Many people in psychology are prejudiced against Skinner. They may have paid too much attention to Skinner as a social philosopher, which I think is not his strong suit. But Skinner's psychology I find very useful, not to control others as so many fear, but to control myself.

One part of the book deals with self-control. Skinner helped me see something I had never realized before. That was how much our environment controls us. One of Skinner's ideas of self-control is to control our behavior by choosing the specific environments we want to be in and avoiding the environments that make it more likely we will emit behavior we don't like. In short, if I don't like the things I find myself doing down at the pool hall, then I had best stay away from the pool hall.

I used to be so dumb that I thought I could be the same person in any environment. I finally realized I was wrong. When I was dealing with my crooked client, the crooked side of me was more likely to show.

The business environment I had been in for fifteen years was wrong for me because I overreacted to it. My job became my number one priority and crowded out my family and my God. Each person has to find environments that are as right for them as possible.

Recently, a friend from the old days, Bob Schmitt, read my first book and wrote me. He told me not to lie to him. He knew I hadn't changed a bit. I thought about what he said and called him the next day. I told him he was right, I hadn't changed; I was still the cantankerous SOB he remembered. But while I hadn't changed, I had changed many of the things I was doing.

It was like my old friend Vince. He still says he is an alcoholic trying to stay sober today. He hasn't changed the fact he is an alcoholic. But he has changed the things he does. One of those things he has changed is that he hasn't had a drink for twenty-three years.

I'm still a hard-charging maniac. But because I'm not in a business I can't handle and I don't have financial pressures that drive me crazy, I'm not such a menace to myself. So this is what I see as being so positive about what Skinner has to say to us. His system of self-control emphasizes our ability to select our environments and so to find those most favorable to the kind of behavior we want to see in ourselves.

This gets at a problem I had never had a good answer to before. That is, "What is the real us?" The answer is that the real us is like a diamond with many facets. Or a coin with two sides. We can see either the good side of

ourselves or the side we don't like to see. Much of what
we see isn't determined by our will power in the situation,
but by the situation we put ourselves in.

If I was dumb enough to move to Las Vegas or Reno, I
know I wouldn't like some of the things I would find myself doing. Would that be the real me? Yes, it would be a
part of me that I recognize as me. But just because I recognize that part of me as me doesn't mean I need to see
very much of it.

See what a positive, helpful idea it is to choose good,
supporting situations and run away from bad, destructive
ones? Isn't that much nicer than trying to be in a bad situation and depending on will power to pull you through?
I think so. And that's a key idea I use in my life today.

The other idea I learned from Skinner on self-control
was the power of internal and external self-reinforce-
ment. When I was in graduate school, I rewarded myself
for fifty minutes of study by giving myself an ice cream
cone. I wrote my Ph.D. dissertation by going to my office
each evening and staying until I had written five pages.
This encouraged production instead of head scratching.
I'm using the same idea this morning. I can quit when I've
written five pages.

My old way of working was to put off studying until I
was forced to. Then once I started and put in a good hour
of study, I would say to my mind, "Ha, I've got you now,
you slippery devil. I'll make you study another hour."
Well, my mind didn't like that deal and rebelled at it. Or I
would try to do things out of a sense of duty. Or use will
power. That doesn't work very well for me. The satisfac-
tion of slowly and steadily working on a job is an eternal
reward to me. The fact that something I do would please
my grandfather is an internal reward for me. But I find I
need a good combination of rewards where I mix both the
external rewards, like time off and ice cream cones, with
the internal ones.

So, on the farm I was facing life as it really was. Before, by living in my fancy suburb, I had removed myself from the breadth of life. I see some of my hippie friends who are astonished at the way they can come into a small town and really communicate with some old character. Their amazement that there are such people tells me they have lived too narrow a life in their middle- or upper-class setting. Just because all the people they were raised with seemed to be hung up on money doesn't mean everybody is. We always have a choice and the choices we make often tell us much more about ourselves than they tell us about our society.

There is a part of each of us that wants others to conform to our ideas. But there is another important part of our society and of each of us that values individuality in ourselves and the people around us. That's why we honor people like the Kennedys, King, Gandhi, Roosevelt, Churchill, Truman. They weren't conformists. I grant that extreme individuality can get us killed by other extremists. Christ and Socrates, Gandhi, King, and the Kennedys found that out. But there is little danger that you or I will be anywhere near that much an individual.

So, I saw that the guys I knew on the farm had long known something I wanted to learn, which was how to be more like I really was and to move away from my false self that was so intent on impressing others. I guess you would call that growing up, a process which for me had been long delayed. It was about time I started.

On the farm, I also took care of another thing that had been long delayed. We had married on a shoestring. I did such a lousy job of handling money that Jackie ended up buying my wedding ring and her own, too. And I couldn't afford to buy her an engagement ring.

Finally, thirteen years later, I saw the stupidity of spending all the money we had spent and her not having a diamond. So it wasn't until we got poor that Jackie got a nice big diamond that she wouldn't have to hide from the other girls.

I was starting to be able to see life on the farm. But some of the strain of worrying about me finally got to Jackie and she had to ask to move to town. It was very hard for me to leave the farm, but Jackie was saying that one of her crucial priorities was involved now, so we moved to town.

Part of the problem was that I had started teaching half time at the university. So Jackie was stuck by herself in the place I wanted to live but wasn't at nearly as much as before.

We came back to the farm but it was never the same. I used to move at a moment's notice with no thought to the consequences. Now I see what they are. When I move, I communicate to the people I leave, "I claim to love you so much but I will go away from you now and hardly ever see you again. That's how much you really mean to me."

6

Jackie

As soon as we sold our suburban house, we found a farmhouse. It was just off the main highway between Minneapolis and Duluth. The nearest town was Wyoming, Minnesota, two miles south.

The house was identical to thousands of other farmhouses in the Midwest, with a long screened porch in the front. In the middle of the porch you entered the huge kitchen. It must have been close to twenty feet square with a small pantry off the back that held a sink and two small cupboards. There were no other cupboards in the whole house.

In a front corner of the kitchen was a sink with a medicine cabinet above. I guessed it must have been where the farmers washed up. I had to guess as I had never been on a farm until I met Jess, and then only to visit for a day or two once in a while.

The house was old. The floors all slanted toward the front of the house. There were some big windows in the kitchen, though, and this made it cheery. The living room was ten by fifteen feet. On the floor against the wall was a huge hot air duct with a grate. Above this was another grate covering a hole in the ceiling. This hole provided the only heat for the three upstairs bedrooms.

Through a door in the living room one walked into a back bedroom. It was a good size, and could hold our king-size bed. To the right was another door. I walked through it into the bathroom. The bathtub was tiny and high. On the right was another door. I was back in the kitchen, having come full circle around the downstairs.

Just left of the bathroom door was a door to the upstairs. The kitchen was a many-doored room. There were creaky wooden stairs leading up. On the top landing, to the left, was a bedroom we picked for little Jess. There was one drafty window in it and no heat. On the right was a larger bedroom. Through it and to the right was the third upstairs bedroom. We put the two little boys in front where the heat hole was. The girls' beds went in the back bedroom. We knew it was going to be cold up there come winter. But it was a home that was big enough, and the rent was only $60 a month plus utilities.

There was a big red barn where the children could play. There were assorted other buildings and up the hill was a chicken house. It looked as if the city girl was going to be rural. Real rural.

The movers had come and gone. We locked up our Edina home.

Now it was time for the whole family to see the house. We turned off the highway and drove through some trees past the horse pasture and up a small rise to our new home. It looked great. The outside was white siding. Paint was flaking off, but it was of small matter. We walked in the door. Barbara, Jess, Jr., and I had spent the previous weeks painting. The kitchen was now sparking white.

If we were going to live on a farm, we were going to look like a farm, I had decided. I bought some inexpensive curtains with bright red ruffles. Roosters marched up and down the material. The stairs to the bedrooms had a fresh coat of serviceable gray. Our furniture was put in place and we were settled. It was August 2, 1962. Six months past the heart attack.

I think a quote from Pearl Buck's book *My Several Worlds* is appropriate here. It helps explain my attitude toward this new life so well: "Though I can live anywhere, be either rich or poor with equal acceptance, I have to have a setting; and if there is not one, I make it."

This is what I set out to do on the farm in Wyoming, Minnesota. I knew what Pearl Buck was talking about. I admired her more than any woman living. She was a sexy lady.

To help our children over the transition from plenty to poverty, from urban to rural, Jess and I took some definite steps. We first decided to buy a horse.

We wound up renting two, and one of these, Beauty, came with a colt running by her side.

A colt! A colt to watch run around the pasture with its mother. Free. How unbelievable. Life was so grand.

I decided to get some chickens. A farm needs chickens. Just a few. Enough for eggs. There was a young farmer who farmed our land on shares for the owner. We had met him the first day. Our farm used to belong to his uncle. We liked this young Bits Osterbauer immediately. He was a rarity. A very wise young man. His wife, Bonnie, was lovely. We loved them both. And they helped us adjust. There are no words for what those two fresh, sweet, honest young people meant to us. Bits had a wonderful wry sense of humor. And Bonnie laughed at his wit harder than anyone else. I consider that true love!

Bits had chickens. Now remember, although my husband had grown up in the country, I was a city girl. It is important to keep this in mind. Jess went across the road to Bits's farm. Bits could spare twelve old hens. Good layers.

Jess and Bits drove into the yard with a big crate full of

twelve fat, white chickens. Bits picked one out of the crate by the legs. Holding the hen upside down, he said, "See, Jackie, see the size of *that*; means they're good layers." I blushed. I'd never seen the rear of a chicken. Bits had a twinkle in his eyes.

I still don't know if the size of *that* has anything to do with being a good layer or not. I wasn't about to give myself away one way or another. We put the hens in the hen house up the hill on the east side of the house. We had two kittens, George and Helen, named for George and Helen Jacques, our dear friends from Prescott, Wisconsin. They, plus our dog, Cocoa, along with the horses and chickens gave me my "setting" as Pearl Buck would say.

Summer was almost over. There was fresh sweet corn from Bits and Bonnie, and I began to bake my own bread. I learned to make sweet cream cake from Bonnie, who would bring me fresh cream by the quart-jarful.

The children were in school. Jess started classes at the University of Minnesota. Fall had arrived. I began to relax. And with relaxation came a deep depression.

I was uprooted. I was living a totally different life. Nothing was familiar. I worked hard at trying to lick my depression. I began to eat, and of course, I began to get heavy. Well, fat is a more truthful word. Soon my chino "country" pants would no longer button.

One fearful day in late fall, Jess got sick. "O God, no!" Jess had always had a touch of asthma. He had been hospitalized for it three or four times in our earlier years. Here it was again. He fought it, and I watched fear spread across his face. Finally he had to stand up to breathe. I called the doctor. We drove the thirty miles to the hospital, where Jess was put in an oxygen tent.

I waited around until his breathing was easier and then started the long drive back to the farm. It was then about 2 A.M., and a crisp, cold fall night. Thousands of stars were shining. I could see my breath. I was clammy with fear. I wondered how asthma affects the heart. As I remembered, asthma was hard on hearts.

"O God, not again. Let him be all right. I can't stay in that farmhouse without Jess. I'm scared. I cannot stand to be alone. And now here I am on this cockamamie farm and Jess is in the hospital. You don't send crosses that we cannot bear, so what is going on? You know how weak I am. Now let up, please. I'm tired." How many times I was going to scream this to God in the future.

I found out I was tougher than I thought. I reached the farmhouse about 3 A.M. I was up at seven. I got the older children off to school. Joe and Mike and I played in the yard. At noon we were all three restless. I'd never saddled a horse before. I thought I could do it. I saddled Nellie. I walked her to the concrete cattle trough and climbed aboard. Joe handed me two-year-old Mike. I put him in front of me. I gave five-year-old Joe a hand. He clambered aboard behind the saddle. We rode Nellie into Wyoming. I tied Nellie up to a big signpost in front of the Country Kitchen. We went inside the cafe for hamburgers, fries, and shakes.

What a contrast. The year before I had been driving the freeways around Edina in my sports car. This year I was on horseback, riding with my children. I honestly thought I liked this life better. I was doing pretty well for a city girl.

That first night alone I woke up with a start. There were horns honking on our land. It was three-thirty in the morning. I threw on a robe and rushed to the front door. A car was driving up the lane tooting the horn. Ahead ran our two horses and the colt. They had gotten out and were on the highway.

What to do? I knew a fence must be down. I thanked the fellow who was playing cowboy with his car and locked the horses in the small pasture in the front of the house. I knew that tomorrow I would have to check the fences. I crawled back into my lonely bed and wept.

The next morning I dressed warmly because it was freezing out. The little boys and I went out to find the hole in the fence. I took a hammer in my hand and put some nails in my mouth. We found the downed fence right away. I took the nails out of my mouth and peeled away part of my lip. It was so cold the nails had frozen to my mouth. I learned a lesson there. I pounded the nails home and fixed the fence. We were near the chicken coop so we went to gather eggs. I had begun to call it "picking eggs" just like all the rest of the farmers. We had been getting nine to twelve eggs a day from our superhens. One day we got thirteen! Today there were no eggs. I couldn't understand it.

Just then Bits drove up, so I asked him. He looked in the coop. "See how white their combs are? Their combs have frozen. They won't lay any more. Better kill 'em and have stewing hens, Jac." Now what does a chicken's comb have to do with laying eggs? I still don't know for sure, but I did have an inkling that the comb on a chicken's head had something to do with egg laying, ridiculous as it seemed.

That afternoon, when Jess, Jr., came home from school I told him about the chickens. "We should kill them and dress them so we can have some good stewed chicken, Jess. Do you think you can help mother chop off the chickens' heads, honey?" I hated even to ask. Young Jess drew himself up tall and walked off for the hatchet. "Just bring one chicken down here. We'll just try to kill one right now, Jess."

Now, how do you kill a chicken? You chop off his head, that's what you do. Jess and I stretched the chicken out on the hard ground. I'd never heard of a chopping block. Whack. Jess hit the neck as hard as he could. The chicken screeched and gave a jerk, slipped from my grasp, and went running wildly around the yard, blood squirting.

We looked with horror at what we had done. I felt like an ax murderess. Nothing to do but finish the job. I ran over and easily caught the bleeding hen. Down on the ground, Jess, Jr. gave another mighty swing. A fresh wound and the chicken took off again, with blood flying, and the chicken still screaming. I caught her again. I looked at my small son. He was white. I knew I would have to finish her off. I took a mighty swing. This time the chicken took off running with her head hanging by a thread. I threw up. Finally, the chicken had bled to death in front of us and toppled over. Never, never again. I fed the eleven hens left in the coop until they died of old age.

Now what does one do with a dead chicken? I remembered from somewhere that you hung them up until the blood was all drained out. I found a rope and took the ghastly mess to the rear of the screen porch where an old hook was set in the ceiling, probably from an old porch swing. I hung the chicken and put a pail under it to catch the drips.

The next day Jess came home from the hospital. He had been in there only three days, but it seemed like ages to us. We settled down to a routine again. Jess drove in to the university every morning and was home by noon or early afternoon each day.

A few days after his return we had a warm spell. Autumn in Minnesota is beautiful. Long, sunny days. Yellow, bronze, and maroon leaves silhouetted against the deep blue sky. Along with the beauty came a terrible odor on our porch. It was the chicken! I had forgotten it. I walked back to the far edge of the porch, and couldn't believe my eyes. I had hung a plump white hen only a few days before. Now there was a skinny white thing that looked five feet long. There wasn't a smell or an odor, there was a stench. Here and there I saw flesh that was an ugly green. We buried the chicken.

The next day our bachelor friend who had rented us Nellie and Beauty called. "Time to check the horses, can I come out?" "Sure, Bud, come on over." Check the horses? What does that mean? I went shopping and left Jess at home with all of the children. It was my Saturday morning at the grocery store, a weekly event.

As I returned from shopping I took the first of two lanes leading into the farm. It was a lovely lane that curved gently past the small horse pasture and up to the house. Ahead I saw Jess and the children standing beside the fence. I realized that Bud must have come.

I rapidly found out what "check" means. Bud had brought a small pony stallion with him. He led the pony into the pasture with the two mares. If the mares are in foal they will rudely reject the amorous stallion. Bud was sure they were both in foal, but Nellie wasn't!

The little stallion approached our big old Nellie. The rope snapped and Bud was dragged bodily around the pasture vainly yelling "Whoa." The tiny stallion was determined to mount Nellie. Nellie was most receptive, even to the point of bending her hind legs to bring herself more on a level with the pony.

Their love was consummated before our wondering eyes, and our children had received their first graphic instruction on the birds and the bees.

Bud was pooped and embarrassed. "Was sure that mare had took. Gosh darn it, I ripped my shirt." I invited Bud in for a snack. After all, he had worked harder than the stallion. Nellie never did "took." I think she was old enough for menopause, anyway.

Soon winter was upon us. We had our first Christmas in the country. It was beautiful. White snow, red barn, blue sky. Upstairs the children were freezing in their beds. We dug out the sleeping bags and they spent the winter in those.

Jess was doing beautifully in school. Finances were tight and he started looking for a job as an instructor at

the university. In the spring he found a job for the following fall on the "Ag" campus of the university. He
would teach speech in the Rhetoric Department.

I hated to see him add teaching to his already loaded
schedule, but facts had to be faced. We were barely
scratching through financially. I still had two small ones
at home all day, and knew of no job that I could take on
to help.

In most stories I have read, the persons involved seem
to live magically without the everyday stress and strain of
a budget. In real life, I find that the nitty-gritty of paying
bills is an ever present, painful fact. We always need a
few more dollars than we have. On the farm we were living on less than half of what we had needed only six
months before. We weren't doing too well. So teaching it
was.

I was gaining weight steadily. From a normal 135 I was
up close to 170. I felt miserable, but when I am worried
or frightened, I eat. I was retaining fluid, also. I was a
mess. I began to feel a lot of self-pity. Self-pity should be
one of the biggest sins there is. It fouls up your mind and
plays hell with your emotions.

I was having another problem, too. I was becoming a
terrible hypochondriac. I would start to doze off at night
and all of a sudden I would sit straight up in bed. I felt as
if I was dying. I began to be afraid to go to sleep. I had
such terrible nightmares. Someone was always lost and I
was searching for him through a huge, rambling house. In
the dream there would be doctors and nurses standing in
every doorway. I frantically searched in my dreams night
after night.

I didn't know it at the time, but I was crumbling slowly.

Earlier I stated that I think the wives of heart attack
patients should face themselves and their emotions early
in the trauma.

I was incapable of doing this partly because I was more

repressed than most, and certainly because every fiber within me was pointing toward removing stress from Jess. As a consequence, I allowed some very deep needs of my own to go unanswered.

At that time in my life I was under a great deal of stress, not only from Jess's heart attack and our change of life-style, but I also was having deep problems caring for our beloved Janet. As a consequence, I had the additional pain of estrangement from her and along with that, estrangement from some of our relatives.

I was torn from the familiar and floundering in a strange situation. In my head the farm was idyllic for Jess and the children. In my heart I was crying for familiar scenes and life-styles.

Looking back, I still would have moved us to the farm. Even knowing what was to follow in our lives, the lessons learned in that brief sojourn are with me still.

Now Jess had chest pains again. They frightened us badly enough to put him into the hospital once more. He came home with nitroglycerin to put under his tongue. And the nights got worse.

I went to a psychiatrist. He agreed that I was very frightened and insecure because of Jess's health and our drastic change in life-style. I had been to a psychiatrist earlier when I had trouble learning to live with our eldest daughter, who has cerebral palsy; it didn't help much. I still cannot write of this, though we have lived with this beautiful child for twenty-three years now. There is something about the suffering of one's own child that is so very painful.

Spring of 1963 arrived. Another season on the farm. The seasons are more pronounced in the country, each with its own beauty. I walked in the woods behind the house. I listened to the birds. I watched the squirrels chasing each other from tree to tree. Barbara was getting prettier every day. She is our second child, born eleven months after Janet.

June arrived and I was hanging clothes in the back yard. Barb came running from behind the barn. "Mama, Mama, come see." I ran. There behind the barn, just wobbling up on shaky matchstick legs, was Beauty's new colt. Barbara's big brown eyes were enormous with the wonder of it all. The other children came running. Joe stared at the wee colt. "Her name is Jellybeans" said our five-year-old. Jellybeans she was. She was still wet, she was so new. We put Jellybeans and Beauty in the new pasture, anxious to see the look on Jess's face when he drove down the lane and saw our new arrival.

This was the season for birth, because the next day our dog Cocoa presented us with eleven puppies. All eleven were healthy, although there weren't enough faucets to go around. We put Cocoa and her litter in the barn. Another surprise for Jess when he came home.

When Jess comes home! How I lived for the moment the car came down the lane. If Jess was very late I became frightened. He was late more and more as his strength returned and he got more interested in school. One day, when he was hours late, he came home to a hysterical wife. I was certain he'd had a heart attack somewhere and no one knew how to find me. From that day on Jess was always considerate enough to call if he was very late.

We had a lot of weekend guests that summer and fall. Once our city friends saw our country home, they came to visit. Some Sundays I fed as many as twenty extra at our huge country table. This was wonderful fun. Horses to ride, woods to roam in, a barn to play hide-and-seek in. A paradise to our city friends. We loved seeing all our good friends. But I noticed that I was getting so tired that the five days between weekends wasn't long enough to recuperate.

In November of that year John Kennedy was killed. Janet and I were glued to the television like many millions of Americans. I didn't know how hard other people were taking this tragedy, but I ceased to function. The horror filled days went by, and I couldn't come out of it. I began to cry at everything. I was terrified of being alone. I couldn't sleep.

Finally, on December 5, I had to face the fact that I could not go on any longer. I told Jess to get me to the hospital. Without any questions he drove me into Minneapolis and I was admitted to a local psychiatric hospital. On admittance I weighed 182 pounds. On Christmas Day, just weeks later, my weight had dropped below 150.

I joined the family for a short time Christmas Day. The strain was too much. I could hardly wait to get back to the hospital.

I got the idea into my head that I would be all right if we could just move back into the city. Dear Jess went along with me and we gave up the farm and moved into a cracker box house on Edgewater in a suburb north of St. Paul. I came home. I couldn't take the strain of the family yet. The doctors began to think I might have a brain tumor. I was admitted to University Hospital. The doctors there were sure I had a tumor. They even felt it was in the cerebellum at the base of the brain. They prepared Jess for my surgery. But before surgery I had a pneumoencephalogram. No tumor!

I didn't know if I was happy or sad. I didn't care. I was living a nightmare. I came home and started seeing a different psychiatrist at the university. I soon realized I couldn't cope with the family yet. I went back into the hospital. I was profoundly depressed and had acute anxiety.

I will not write of the many weeks ahead. They were hell for me and even greater hell for Jess and the children. I, at least, had tranquilizers and anti-depressants. They had to take it cold turkey. In June I finally got a good enough grip on myself to return home. It was great to see the children and Jess. My anxiety for him was diminished somewhat and life began to return to normal.

I had one huge regret; we had left the farm. We saw Bits and Bonnie each hunting season for a few more years. But we never drove back to look at our farmhouse.

The next fall we bought a house just a few blocks from the St. Paul campus where Jess was now working full time. He had earned his master's degree the past June and was halfway to his Ph.D., just two years after he started back to school. Janet and Barbara were in junior high school. Jess, Jr., was now in sixth grade. Joe was in first grade and Mike was home with us. Life was indeed becoming quieter.

7

Jess

We moved from the farm to a small house in a suburb north of St. Paul. Our stay in the house on Edgewater was mostly hanging on—enduring. It wasn't much of a home compared to the farm. But it was easy to manage and didn't demand a sixty-mile-a-day round trip to school. Jackie was in the hospital a lot. The kids and I were lost without her in the family. We tried to help each other as well as we could, but it was a lonesome time for all of us.

I was teaching speech half time at the St. Paul campus of the university. I was trying to find a new way to make a living.

My memory of what went on in the way of feelings during my first years on campus is very dim. I had just come out of the tornado of doing all the wrong things in my business and was trying all kinds of new things. The feelings I had about those days were pretty much beneath the surface and unknown to me, then and even now. More than anything, I think I was buying time—time to find a better way, more fitting to me.

Many people write to tell me they have left the rat race of business just as I did and have given up material prosperity for a simple, rural life of poverty. I think they miss the whole point of my story in their comments. I went back to the farm because it was comfortable to me. I left the advertising business because it was wrong for me. There is a rat race in university life, too. Lots of the psychology professors I knew were in their offices late at night trying to get ahead while their wives raised their families without them.

So there isn't any one right way for everyone. Jim Larkin must be one of the busiest lawyers I know, yet he is also by far one of the easiest to be around. I now do five times as much as when I was in the advertising business, but that's because this work is more right for me. But all of teaching isn't a ball. There are parts of teaching that hurt so much. The problems in finishing up at the end of a class are so hard that I'm worthless as a husband and father the last two weeks of each quarter.

And there isn't in my life the idyllic calm, happy, peaceful existence some people choose to see. I'm just another human being trying to find my way.

Right now I grant I've got lots of ideas I didn't have before. Where did those ideas come from? They came partly from those early days in university life where I was just blindly reaching out on faith trying all kinds of things to find which of them "fit like a glove." And to find which things I should put down.

About all I have to tell you concerning those first years is what I did and a little about how I felt. Much of how I felt came later out of what I did then.

My boss in the Rhetoric Department was Ralph Nichols. Ralph didn't even ask me if I had ever taken a speech course (I hadn't). I told him of my experiences organizing a couple of Toastmasters clubs, speaking professionally and consulting with a prominent speaker on material. He thought that qualified me to teach. He wasn't worried about my academic qualifications. But then, he always was an unorthodox man.

I used a number of ideas from the B. F. Skinner book I mentioned earlier to teach my speech classes. Almost all my students were frightened. So the first two weeks I tried to help put out most of their fear. They thought they were poor speakers and they were afraid of being punished. I tried to show them their individual strengths so they could see they had a start and could just work on improvement. They didn't like to make speeches. As soon as they sat down after a talk, I tried to give them as many positive rewards as I could by praising what they had done well and only then pointing out some weakness they could work on to be even better.

I started teaching those first few weeks in my advertising man's clothes. Most advertising men were already dressing like peacocks at a time when everyone else was still wearing gray or black. So I had beautiful clothes. But I felt uncomfortable standing in front of my students so overdressed. I started wearing an old Harris tweed coat that was nearly worn out and a pair of wash-and-wear pants and I felt much more at ease.

During the middle of the first quarter, a speaker came to our campus to advocate the use of student evaluation of the teacher. I thought it was a good way to find out the strengths and weaknesses of my teaching. At the end of the quarter, after I had made out my students' grades, I asked them to tell me what they liked and didn't like about my class. The answers were not to be signed.

I was startled to read the papers. My nineteen- and twenty-year-old students were exceptionally perceptive about what was going on in our classroom. They told me I was doing fairly well for a new teacher but I was very inconsistent in my grading. About a third of the students made that point, so they had probably been talking about it to each other. But without class evaluation I would never have known it.

I looked at the grades I had given and saw that my students were probably right. There were two or three students in each of the two classes of eighteen who were pretty girls or personable guys. They gave a good speech or two at the beginning of the course and from then on I gave them good grades all the time. I think they could have read out of the phone book and still gotten a good grade from me.

I went to work on my grading that next quarter. During each speech I tried to forget my impressions of previous speeches and listen to that one. At the end of the next quarter I had cut the inconsistency of grading criticisms drastically and from the third quarter on I didn't get that criticism any more.

There were a number of other suggestions the students made on how they felt the course could be improved. Most of those suggestions I acted on. And each quarter, the class did a better job with the final two or three speeches.

My experience with class evaluations is a good example to me of how hard it is for me to be honest about myself. It is easy for me to be "honest" about the other man's faults and problems. But what is that kind of honesty worth when I can't be honest about my own weaknesses and problems?

At that time the only person who was honest with both herself and me was my wife. Since that time I have been slowly building up a number of relationships with people who will be honest with me. But that deep honesty can only come from people who are being honest with themselves, too, or else I find they are just dumping their own anger at themselves and the world on me in the name of honesty.

My friend Vince, who lives such a fine life, said to me recently that he had a very precious asset in living the AA program. Not only did he have an evening meeting or two a week he could go to, he also had built up honest relationships with about a hundred people so he could go to any one of them when his thinking got screwed up. His friends could and would gently tell him the truth.

I was so struck by that because I wondered how many people have built such good relationships that they get true but gentle and loving honesty? What honesty most of us find from others is not honesty, but just anger.

The emotional rewards of teaching helped me get over my nervousness with my students. As I saw that I could be a part of their becoming much better speakers in a happy way I was much less fearful about what I was doing and began to develop some confidence in myself.

I had always needed people so desperately. I needed the feeling that I was an individual and that I mattered to people. I found those things in teaching. By giving me so much of what I needed it helped calm me down a little. And it helped along the healing process of my soul that really started when I was struck down with that heart attack. I had to be faced with losing everything, even my own life, before I would look at what my heart and my soul were trying to tell me.

I was far more nervous and frightened with my fellow faculty members than I was with my students. I wanted to make a good impression. I desperately needed to be liked and accepted in the group. But my fear of them and their fear of me and each other made it impossible for me to build any deep relationships. So far now I have been in three different college departments. I haven't had but a couple of close relationships with anyone in those groups. The fact that I have had some close relationships with faculty members outside the departments I have been in suggests that most of the problem is in me. And I'm working on it.

Each noon many of the professors and young instructors in our department had lunch together at a big table in the faculty dining room. I wanted to be liked and tried to fit in. Anytime anyone does that he is asking for trouble.

In a way I was saying to people, beat on me. Before long, some of the faculty members obliged. Some of the things that happened may seem like dumb little things now, but they sure did hurt then.

I remember one day some of the guys were sitting around and someone asked what kind of bird we would like to be if we could be a bird. The others said hummingbirds or robins. When my turn came I said I wanted to be an eagle. They all laughed at my choice and I was hurt. It was funny and the choice was very like me. But it was also very like me to hate to be laughed at.

Another time we were talking of some Big Social Issue. I made some comment that I suppose was disrespectful and one of the young instructors said, "Well, that's about what you would expect from an advertising man." So I got hurt but enjoyed it. I must have because I kept going back for more.

This was my second year in college. I could handle halftime teaching and my course work in psychology quite well. So I didn't have many health problems that year.

I bought a deer rifle. I had hunted deer with a shotgun that used slugs my first season. But now I had the little money, the time, and the friends so that a deer rifle made sense. It was just two years after my heart attack. It was a funny thing, too. I wouldn't use that rifle but two or three days a year, but just walking by my gun rack was like a one-minute vacation each day.

There are all kinds of interesting psychological interpretations of the significance of guns to men. Some of those interpretations may be right. All I know was that I was trying to save my life. My narrow intellectuality had almost killed me. I saw I couldn't figure everything out. In some things I needed to feel my way. I feel now that an intellect unbalanced by feelings is a cold and destructive force. It may be beautiful to some people. But it is a horror to me—and for me. There are many mysteries in life that this dumb Norwegian isn't ever going to be able to figure out. So there are a lot of things I will accept as just that, mysteries.

Hunting is one of those mysteries. Why it means so much to me I can't begin to understand. When I tried to control it completely, I was so miserable that I made life miserable for the people around me. Right now my family and I are trying to find some balance in the way I handle it and an acceptance of it that can work. I think we are all doing better and hunting is quickly becoming much less of an obsession with me.

A few years ago I was so obsessed with hunting that one day as I was starting on a weekend hunting trip, I found myself already planning the next trip. I knew that there was no way this trip I was on (or any real trip) could live up to my dream and my obsession. Now I'm smart enough to know that's plenty weird. What I'm trying to do as far as hunting is concerned is work at my life from all sides so that I have less need for obsessions. Hunting has progressed to the point for me after eight years where I can go and enjoy the horseback ride and the good company and not be frustrated when I'm not successful. But I've still got a way to go.

Fishing used to be an obsession with me. I now go only when it seems as though that's the best thing to do at the moment. And I spend almost as much time watching my sons or my friends fish and talking with them as I do fishing myself. And I don't weigh, measure, or count the number of fish I catch. That's why I have hopes for hunting becoming more and more an enjoyable recreation.

I guess one of the reasons I digressed so on hunting is that I know how painful a topic it is to many women and some men. I know, too, that the topic might be painful to you that it might be difficult not to let emotion rule and to shut out my story because it is so hard to have sympathy for the hunting urge part of it. But so far, that's part of me.

I find most coronary personalities have obsessions of

one kind or another. What is the difference between an obsession and a genuine deep interest? I think there is a driven quality to an obsession that blinds us to everything else. That's why it serves us so well, it blots out all our worries and problems. Fishing used to be an obsession. I was so preoccupied with it that it drove everything else out of my mind. I was constantly thinking about some new tactic or new piece of equipment that I was sure would solve all my problems. It got so I was loaded like a pack mule with spare equipment I might need when fishing.

Now I put on a light pair of cheap plastic waders, put a small box of flies in my pocket, and carry just a light canvas creel and my rod. I enjoy the sun on the water, the company, and laugh at the fish I miss. That's the difference between an obsession and a hobby.

If you recognize an obsession of yours from my description, it doesn't mean you have to give it up. Our obsessions serve needs and we usually don't give up the obsession until the need it serves is satisfied some other way. So the point of the obsession is to see it as a clue there is some deep need in you that should be recognized and met. As you do this, the obsessive quality of something drops away because you don't need it.

Many of my former obsessive hobbies, I have now found I don't even like. I used to play medium stakes poker one night a week. I haven't played poker five times in the past ten years. I find I don't want to take money from my friends and I don't want to spend time with strangers. I brought my golf clubs to Montana but I haven't touched them since I came here.

It is a real relief to me to be rid of so-called recreations that I didn't really like. Now I can do what I do like and flow with the rhythm of the seasons. I don't need to spend much time looking forward to anything.

There's snow now as I'm writing this, so we're having a good time skiing. When it gets warm in March, I'll start riding and fishing will come in the summer and hunting in the fall. But all those other things are ahead of me. What is here now is the snow and the skiing. Pearl Buck says she thinks we have robbed the seasons of some of their charm by having sweet corn and strawberries almost year round.

Abouth this time I made another crucial move in my efforts to find a new way to make a living. Whit Longstaff, my Ph.D. adviser, urged me to write my dissertation on something in advertising or market research. That way I would know more about the topic than my committee members and I could do it more easily and surely. Whit wanted me to get through. He saw my Ph.D. as something to use all my life, not just in the few years I was working on it. He saw that nothing I could do my Ph.D. dissertation on was especially significant compared to getting the degree and working the rest of my life on the topics that most interested me. So he told me to do my dissertation on a problem in advertising research so I could complete it quickly and well.

Whit helped me another way. He excused me from any more course work in advertising or market research because of my experience. This allowed me to concentrate on other areas of psychology, which was so helpful because I could take lots of learning theory.

So that academic year (1963-64) I taught half time, took course work for my Ph.D. and worked on my Ph.D. topic.

In the spring of 1964, Ralph Nichols called me in and offered me the direction of the first course in the freshman writing program. He didn't ask me if I had a lot of courses in English (again, I hadn't). I didn't feel I was qualified but he said that my journalism training could be used as a justification. He recommended me for a full-time teaching job and the leadership of the fifteen people who were teaching the freshman writing course.

I got the job and so the next year I taught full time,

finished my course work, and worked on completing my Ph.D. project. It was a busy time. But the teaching of writing and the course leadership went very well for me. All I had to do was carry out the program set up by the man who had had the job before me. Dick Horberg was one of the most gifted writing teachers I had ever met. His program and his friendship made that part of my job easy.

I found that I enjoyed teaching writing even more than teaching speech. All the problems my freshmen writing students were facing in their papers were problems I had had as a writer. I had learned ways to cope with those problems and could share them. I wasn't horrified at my students' problems, and I didn't see them as evidence of their low moral or social state. They were just writing problems.

I also saw that I needed to give good assignments and give them carefully, and always to work in a positive way with my students. When I taught this way I could take fifty-two first-quarter freshmen in their hated writing course and get all of them to turn in their seven assignments on time and pass the course. None would get sick of me or drop out of school.

My success left me with two troublesome feelings. The first was a sense of how responsible I was for failures in my students. I saw that when I gave an assignment poorly, my students did poor work. Ever since then I haven't been able to duck my failures in the classroom and other places so well because of the experience of seeing my big part in those failures.

The whole process of teaching writing turned out to be pleasant for me and my students, so almost all of them came each day and we did without taking attendance. The class was one I too enjoyed going to each day. I found teaching, to use my heart attack roommate's words, "fit me like a glove." I liked what I was doing. My students liked what I was doing. Based on the way things were going, that fall of 1964 I started looking for houses for sale as I drove back and forth between the two campuses of the University of Minnesota.

We moved into our house on Dudley Avenue, just five blocks off the St. Paul campus, in December. The kids had to switch schools for the fourth time in five years, which was horrible, but they took it without complaining because they knew we had to have a home. And Dudley was it. It was the place where we would try to reestablish ourselves in a new way of life.

Jackie's and my expectations of what we were going to find in a college community were all wrong. We thought our tree-lined street of old houses would be a serene and happy place. Because we expected way too much, we were horrified by the reality. There were suicides there. And lots of very suppressed and hidden anger that kept leaking out in funny ways.

Yet, much of the problem was our fault. The worst thing I can do is to expect something of you, because that locks you in. "You are not in this world to live up to my expectations," says Dr. Frederick Perls, the Gestalt psychotherapist. By putting our expectations on our small community we were blinded to the good and literally forced people to be less than their best.

Bill and Ann Bulger lived a few blocks from us but we were scared of them because their house was so big and imposing. I'm sure Bill and Ann will laugh when they read this because they can't imagine anyone being scared of them. They are the gentlest people in the world. But we were coming at the situation all screwed up. So we couldn't help but have some problems.

The people around us were as kind as people can be. The Landises, Vireos, Schaffers, and Brodericks were gentle and helpful. But because of our stupidity we were looking for the impossible. We could always move. That had worked before and could again.

I passed my written Ph.D. exams so then I could take

my oral. If I passed that, I could submit my dissertation in the first part of the summer session. Then I would be through.

During April and May I tore into writing my Ph.D. dissertation. I went to my office after supper and wrote five pages as fast as I could and then came home. Most nights I made my quota of pages. In six weeks I was done with it.

By the end of spring quarter in 1965 my Ph.D. was completed except for the formalities. My teaching was, of necessity, only getting part of my effort, but it was going well enough. I was promoted from an instructor to an assistant professor for the following year.

On the St. Paul campus that spring quarter, they had their annual spring celebration with a faculty member chosen as king. It was an honor, and from the different nominees I was elected. So three years after my heart attack, in my driving way I had rebuilt a new kind of life.

Maybe I should say I had built a new version of the old life because I had been running from the time I started back at the university. My running had accomplished a lot, but it didn't represent as much change as outside circumstances might suggest. I had just done my running in a new environment and I would have to pay for that.

I had made a drastic improvement in my life in one way. I was finally doing what I was good at. And I was in an environment that was more rigid for me and less dangerous than my business environment had been. I could stir up almost as much trouble in university life as before, but I could get out of it lots quicker and more easily.

After that big year I had put in, it was time for a vacation. I taught the first five weeks of summer session and graduated. We took off for a five-week camping vacation together. I had built a huge car top carrier. We had a tent for Jackie and me to sleep in with two cots and a Coleman lantern to read by. We had a tent trailer for the five kids, who at that time ranged in age from five to fifteen.

We had started camping ten years earlier with a few blankets and a borrowed tent. It was years of cooking over campfires before Jackie even had a Coleman stove. Our rare times of real peace in our family were when we were camping. For some people camping is flies, fights, and disillusionment. For us it was always peaceful times together. It was also about the only time I stopped running. I could spend hours just sitting and watching the fire and drinking tea with Jackie. This five-week trip, then, was nothing new. It was just an extension of what we had done for years. We and our outfit were all tested out.

We camped overnight in the Badlands, which we had always wanted to do. It was like camping on the moon. We spent two weeks camped on Sheridan Lake in the Black Hills, which was as long as we were allowed to camp there. Then we went to the Tetons for two weeks and camped at Pelican Bay on Jackson Lake.

Barbara had a hot appendix when we made camp and she was operated on in Jackson, Wyoming, the next day. We planned to stay anyway. She just missed out on our mornings of hauling firewood for our big bonfires in the evenings. Barbara had her stitches out at Yellowstone Park nurse's office as we were on our way to Bozeman to camp at Bozeman Hot Springs and fish the Gallatin.

The year before I had been offered a job at Eastern Montana College in Billings, but that fell through. At Montana State University in Bozeman I saw a place I would like to live. I talked to some of the people at the university about coming to work there.

After as happy a time as a family can have, we returned home. There hadn't been one fight or argument in the five weeks. But when I tried to go back to regular living, I discovered that I hadn't really changed my life much in three years.

I came back to campus and went at everything hard. I started forcing myself and my ideas on people. In class I was basically happy with myself. But I set out to change

the rest of the world. I don't recall all the things I did
wrong partly because then I wasn't paying as close attention to what I did as I do now. I know one thing I did was
to take the good things I could do in the classroom and
make a big ego scene out of them. This understandably
made some of my fellow professors mad. I also wrote a
report on the beneficial use of class evaluation. It showed
some of the good things my students were saying about
me, and that was hard for people to swallow, too. I sent
the report to our dean. He felt it should be reprinted and
sent to the whole faculty and I should speak at a faculty
meeting.

I'll never forget that meeting. Five professors came.
Four attacked me for thinking what students said was of
any value. Actually, they were mad at me as they had a
right to be. I learned a lot about myself from that meeting. My guts hurt so bad as I stood on that stage facing
those angry people.

Sure I can justify everything in that report. But it was
too damn selective to be true. Why didn't I tell about my
failures? I was putting myself in the best possible light
and my colleagues in the worst.

When I write my book on teaching: *How I Fail as a
Teacher—Each Day,* I will tell the truth. Because even
though I will speak mostly of my failures, the good will be
there between the lines and will communicate itself without words. So that will be the whole truth. What I did in
St. Paul was a big lie. Not only will God get me for that, I
lived through a touch of hell as I paid for my mistake.

But as Vince says, "We need our mistakes." The bigger
the better. The more we hurt, the less chance we will
make that mistake again.

So I won't make any more speeches to the faculty
about what a great teacher I am.

By spring I had things so screwed up again that getting
overtired, overworked, and sick was the only way out. I
woke up in the middle of one night with a terrible nausea.

I staggered to the bathroom and slumped over the toilet bowl. All I could say when Jackie came in was, "Call the doctor." I was conscious all the time but unable to respond to the people around me. Our neighbor, a doctor, came and took my pulse and listened to my heart. The rescue department came and gave me oxygen, and then they took me to the hospital. The next day I felt weak but all right. A stay in the hospital usually helps me break a pattern of running. I calmed down some and my fellow professors took my classes for me until the end of the quarter.

We decided to take the whole summer off and go to Absarokee, Montana. A year earlier we had bought a lot there with the idea of building a summer home on it.

We spent the summer camping in a house at the edge of Absarokee. It didn't work very well. I guess it might have been that we were trying both to live in Absarokee and to camp at the same time. Maybe they don't mix. Also, I think Jackie and I could see that even though we had changed the circumstances of our life, things were a lot the same. The newness of teaching had worn off. We were faced with something Jackie has said to me so often as I try frantically to manipulate life, "Jess, there is only one thing you can do with life, that's live it."

We had changed everything we could change. And we could see those changes were right and good. Teaching was giving me the emotional rewards I needed. I was doing things naturally and easily "because they fit like a glove," and I was being promoted every year with good pay raises.

My problem was serenity. I found that out and discovered the program to work toward it through an organization called Emotions Anonymous which was patterned after Alcoholics Anonymous.

I found a warmth and acceptance for me in that small group of people in a church basement in St. Paul that I had never felt before. I had read about acceptance and heard it talked about hundreds of times. But it didn't mean anything to me until I actually experienced acceptance.

One night at an EA meeting I asked, "How come, when I come to this meeting, it's like coming into a warm room on a cold winter day? It's like coming home to that perfect home we all long for." And Ann B. looked at me with those big blue eyes of hers and said, "That's because we accept you, Jess." And that's one of the sad, funny things about that program. People who desperately need help themselves can be very healing for others. Their own needs and hurts don't keep them from healing others. In fact, their own hurts are the very thing that helps them heal others.

I now see this as a concept that I am working on called Mutual Need Therapy. One of the two founders of AA said that there can be no communication between two people unless there is a recognition of their mutual need for each other. And I see that unless there is real communication between people they die one way or another.

Each week, as I went to those meetings, I would have to tell my story. I was able to start looking at the days I was living. And I was helped by the honesty of the fellowship to be more honest about my own feelings about myself.

The warmth of their acceptance for me was like the warmth of the sun. Only the sun can open the bud of a plant so you can see the flower. So did the warmth those people felt for me help me to open myself to them and to myself.

When I was thinking of the move to Montana, one man at the meeting told of his attempts to solve a drinking problem by moving from one place to another—the geographic cure. He told me, "Remember, Jess, wherever you go, there you are."

In Emotions Anonymous, each meeting is opened with the Serenity Prayer, which says:

> God, grant me the serenity
> To accept the things I cannot change;
> Courage to change the things I can;
> And the wisdom to know the difference.

Jackie and I seemed to have plenty of courage to change things. We had changed everything we could change. But I was awful short on serenity. In fact, I didn't have any. I couldn't accept myself as I was. I couldn't accept my wife as a unique woman. Much of the time I wanted her to be a Norwegian man, and yet I didn't want that either. I wanted my kids to be kids when I wanted them to be, and machines when I might be inconvenienced by them. And I wanted to be able to bug anyone around me without them retaliating in any way. I wanted to be able to put the worst construction on every one of their actions and yet have them treat me sweetly.

At one meeting of Emotions Anonymous, I asked out loud why I didn't have more deep personal relationships. The words were no more than out of my mouth in that warm and accepting group than I realized I didn't want close emotional relationships.

I was able to see that I wanted my friends at arm's length. I wanted to take them off the shelf and play with them when I wanted. Then I wanted to put them back on the shelf to wait there until I was ready to play with them again a week, a month, or a year later. I saw that I wouldn't want to be a friend of mine. I saw that I didn't have close emotional relationships because I didn't want them.

By having many friends I could also be spared real closeness with any of them. My whole system was set up to protect me from closeness to others. I think the reason for it was that I was afraid of the self-awareness and self-knowledge that close relationships bring. Those relationships are like a mirror held up to ourselves and it is so terrible for me to see some of the things that are in me. No wonder I didn't have close friends.

The fact I was able to see this and admit it in that special climate of that EA meeting raised my hopes that I might be ready to put aside some of my defenses against closeness.

I also got some sense of what serenity means at those meetings. It is my hope now that through more and more acceptance I can find the deep serenity I see in one man, Vince, an old AA member here in Bozeman.

I don't worry nearly as much about the courage to change things. I seem to have quite a bit of courage. If anything, I might try to change some things that shouldn't or needn't be changed. But, oh, that serenity, how I need that. And how short I am of it. Fortunately, I was to experience some serenity fairly soon during a time that was literally life and death for me.

8

Jackie

As time went by in our *own* home in St. Paul the children grew. Jess began teaching full time on the St. Paul campus just five blocks from us.

And my emotional problems were pretty much under control. I had finally begun to accept the insecurity I felt because of Jess's health. It is hard to explain the terror I felt and lived with daily. That terror raised all sorts of hell with my body. I ached and pained a lot. I still sat up in bed in the middle of the night gasping for breath, heart pounding. But I learned to laugh at myself and go back to sleep. The older children were making a hard adjustment to their fourth school in five years. They were frightened, too. The minute they came home from school they would call out, "Mom, Mom." I saw to it that I was always there to answer.

The first year on Dudley Avenue in St. Paul was uneventful. Life seemed to be settling down.

Our second year began with a bang. Our youngest son,

Mike, was sick one night. I was tired. I put him in bed between Jess and me. Sometime later I was aware that Jess got out of bed. I didn't think much of it. Shortly I heard a loud thump. I ran to the bathroom. Jess was prone, face down, his head and shoulders half resting on the toilet seat. I touched him. He was clammy. "Get help" was all he could groan.

I ran downstairs and called the operator for the rescue squad and reached Jess's doctor, who said he would send an ambulance. I then called a neighbor who was a doctor at the University Health Service. He was the first to arrive. He listened to Jess's heart, felt his pulse, and was visibly shaken. Just then I heard sirens.

The children were up and milling about. Police and the fire department rescue squad poured into the house. It was 3 A.M. Lights were popping on up and down the street.

I made the boys stay in bed. Cruel, but necessary. I could only handle so much. I sent Barbara downstairs to call Audrey, a dear neighbor who always helped in a pinch. The firemen trooped upstairs with oxygen. They rolled Jess over and we put pillows under his head and upper torso. They began to give him oxygen. He was still breathing.

The ambulance arrived. More sirens and whirling red lights. They carried Jess downstairs in a seat fashioned by their hands. Downstairs they put him on a stretcher and covered him up warmly. Throughout all of this confusion I found that I couldn't speak. My mouth was so dry that my lips stuck to my teeth and my tongue was stuck to the roof of my mouth. I grabbed a bottle of Pepsi from the refrigerator and would first wet my dry throat with a swig of Pepsi each time I wanted to speak.

I told the children not to worry and ran out to the waiting ambulance. An attendant was in back with Jess. They didn't want me there with him. I climbed in front with the driver. I kept looking back through the window at Jess. The attendant would give the OK signal with his hand.

We arrived at the hospital. When they pulled the stretcher out Jess looked 100 per cent better. The clammy, wet perspiration was all but gone. His face had more color. I relaxed a little. Jess was put to bed. An EKG machine was brought in. I sat in the waiting room until morning. The doctor came and said all was well. Jess showed no signs of another heart attack. His EKG looked good. What was wrong then? The doctor didn't know.

For the first time I heard mention of heart surgery. "There is a new operation, just developed, and it looks good. If Jess keeps on having trouble I may recommend it," said the doctor. I didn't pay much attention. I think I didn't want to hear about it just then.

My days became a familiar routine. Home, children, and hospital. One night I didn't feel like going home after I had visited Jess so I stopped off at our neighbor's house, the home of the good doctor who had rushed to our aid that night.

I told him that all was well with Jess. As far as our family doctor could see he had not had a heart attack; our doctor didn't seem to see much wrong with him. Dick got a guarded look on his face and I could see his professional manner enfolding him like a cloak.

"Look, Dick, you were there before anyone. You didn't like what you saw. Now I *need* to *know*. Off the record, what do you think?"

"I don't like it," he said. "Don't let those doctors lull you to sleep. From what I heard and what I saw, Jess was nearly a dead man in that bathroom. You watch him carefully, and you get him to a hospital quickly if this ever happens again."

It is not easy for a doctor to drop his professional mask and be a friend. I went home strangely relieved. I had seen Jess in the bathroom, too. I knew that Dick was closer to the truth than our family doctor, who saw him hours after the fact.

Jess came home once again. I remembered Dick's warning. I watched him carefully. I tried to be calm.

Soon my physical problems reared their ugly heads. I began to have aches and pains and then one night a monster of a pain hit right in my middle. I went to the bathroom to find I was bleeding internally.

Panicked, I felt that I couldn't get sick. But I was. The diagnosis was ulcer. I spent a few weeks in the hospital. Nothing showed on X ray.

Did I have an ulcer? It occupied my mind for quite a while.

Looking back from this vantage point, I've decided that I didn't have one. I truly believe that my emotions were so tense I had all the symptoms and was very close to one, but I haven't been troubled now for quite a few years. I think that I had just "had it." Something had to give, and because I couldn't learn how to relax I had to pay a price. But Jess and the children were paying, too. I didn't like that. I was determined to calm down and start taking life easier.

As our second spring on Dudley arrived, Jess was finishing his work on his Ph.D. We had one earth-shaking scare during that time. Jess was writing his Ph.D. thesis in a little library tucked away on the top floor of the Fish and Wildlife Building on the St. Paul campus. One day we heard sirens. The whole family trooped over to the campus to see where the fire was. Lordy, the Fish and Wildlife Building. We stood and perspired as the firemen did their work. They got the fire out without burning up Jess's papers.

We began to plan our summer. Jess was not working this summer so we planned to live in a tent in Montana. It would be fun to leave our cares behind us and live like gypsies.

First, of course, we all went to Jess's graduation, so proud to see him become Dr. Lair. We had a psychologist in the family. A psychologist as a husband and father is just like any other husband and father, though. They don't dare try to play psychologist with their own families. I know we'd clobber Jess if he tried to use any of his newfound wisdom on us. We know him too well!

The trailer was loaded, the house was rented for the summer. It was time to leave for Montana. I awoke at 6 A.M. and sang out, "Who's ready to see the mountains?" I was answered by a chorus of children shouting, "Me, Me, Me."

The summer before, after I had returned home from my long stay at University Hospital, we had been tenting in Montana for five weeks. We spent that time in usual Lair fashion: a great mixture of fun and pathos. Jess, Jr., found a buffalo skull, which we have hanging in our home right now. Michael fell down a mountainside and split his forehead. The children caught many fish. They learned to lasso from an Indian agent camped next to us. Barbara had her appendix removed at Jackson Hole, Wyoming. The rangers there adopted her and visited her daily. We went to Yellowstone Park and saw Old Faithful erupt. Joe met Mrs. Goodhue, his favorite teacher, in Jackson Hole, and she bought him a cowboy hat. I sincerely hoped that *this* trip would be exciting, but that all appendixes would stay cool. And that no one would fall off any mountains.

We arrived in Absarokee, Montana, the next day and pulled into Aunt Julia Eggen's yard. Our plan to "tent" around Absarokee seemed doomed. There were no campgrounds. We decided to see if we could rent a house. There were no furnished homes for rent. We rented a three-bedroom unfurnished home instead. It was the last house on Main Street as you drove toward the Beartooth mountain range. A kitchen window looked down the valley toward the mountains.

I had only had my one and a half years in a small town when we were on the farm, but I had learned enough to know that the whole town of Absarokee knew we were there.

I learned later that many people kept waiting for the truck to arrive with the doctor's furniture. There was no furniture coming. We moved in with our camp gear. We slept on the floor in sleeping bags. All except Barbara, that is. Barb is the enterprising Lair. She discovered that the closet in her bedroom was built about two feet off the floor to accommodate two built-in drawers. Barbie slid the doors back and tucked her sleeping bag into the closet. She had a snug little bed and could shut the closet door when she was mad at Janet.

Barbara had turned into a "swan" and the boys of Absarokee were soon hanging around the house. I did not handle this well. I was not prepared for adolescence and like many parents was overly strict with the first one. (Janet is our first, but her handicap pushed Barbara, just eleven months younger, to the lead in the race through adolescence.) I nagged and I laid down impossible rules and acted as though Barb was about to elope with every fourteen-year-old swain that appeared. How foolish I was. But I learned, at least I learned.

By the fourth of July I had had it again, trying to keep house in a house that was not a home was impossible. I did not have my setting. We packed up and headed for the Tetons for a week. We made camp by the shore of Jackson Lake. Now I had my setting. I began to feel better.

The first day there, a young couple came walking hand in hand down the dirt road swinging a fish behind them. "I wonder, sir, if you could tell me if this is a trout?" asked the young man in an obvious New York accent. Jess looked, his eyes twinkled, "Well, no, I think that's a sucker." Quick as a shot the fellow came back with, "Well, how about calling it a bugle-mouth trout."

So began our acquaintance with the delightful young

couple, Fred and Nancy Silverstein, straight from the streets of New York City. Fred was a senior at Columbia Medical School. He had a Buck knife and a brand-new fly rod and he was in love with the West. Nancy was an artist, and we have two pastels that she did at the Tetons hanging in our home.

Within an hour of our meeting, Fred had learned how to tie his own flies from watching Jess. That night they went fishing at a hole in the Snake River that Jess knew about. Fred's newly tied fly was the one the fish were taking and Fred was soon whooping with joy as he caught fish after fish. My competitive husband smiled tightly and frantically tried to catch up. Even fishing is a contest to his coronary soul. Fred caught the most and we dubbed the hole Silverstein's Pool.

That night and for many more nights we built a big fire and talked with Fred and Nancy until the wee hours. Jess named Fred "Silverstein the Medical Machine," and began to try to convince Fred that there really was quite a bit of medicine practiced west of New York City. It was all in fun, but Fred really loved the West. He and Nancy now live in Seattle—about as far west as you can practice medicine in the continental United States.

The day after Fred and Nancy left, Jess and I left the children and drove west to Bozeman, Montana, and the state university. We had decided that we must move to Montana. We loved the mountains, we loved our Montana relatives, in short, our hearts were here.

Jess put in applications for jobs in the English, Commerce, and Psychology departments. On the St. Paul campus of the University of Minnesota he was teaching freshman writing and speech. His doctorate was in psychology, but his practical working life had been spent writing and speaking. Hence the odd profession for a psychologist. We returned to Absarokee with high hopes of a position at Montana State University.

I had to get back to Minneapolis. I found my lack of a setting too depressing to last long in Absarokee. I felt rootless and anxious living in my shell of a house. We pulled out August 1 and headed for Clearwater Lake near Annandale, Minnesota. Bob and Marlys Pritchard were building a campground and trailer park there. We intended to live in our tent trailer there until we could get back into our own home on September 1. The rain and cold of a wet August caused us to do a wildly extravagant thing. We put a down payment on a thirty-eight-foot two-bedroom house trailer and move it into Clearwater Forest. We were warm and dry and content once more.

September 1 we moved back to Dudley. We spent our weekends, however, in our trailer on Clearwater Lake. We fished and hiked in September, hunted game birds and deer in the fall, and ice-fished in the winter. The trailer became our retreat from city life, which was rapidly losing its enchantment for us now that we had teenagers.

Jess was once again back into the hurly-burly of university life. Before Jess became a teacher, I, like many outsiders, assumed that college professors led a quiet, peaceful, non-competitive life. This stereotype is simply not true as far as I can see. We knew many harried, cutthroat people in the business world, but we had seen nothing to compare with the infighting that so often goes on in university life. Many of those benign-looking white-haired college professor types would "eat their own young," to quote a dear professor friend of ours. Life is truly the same all over, with no place to find serenity if you don't carry your own serenity inside yourself.

Barbara and Janet started high school and Jess, Jr., was in eighth grade the fall of '66. Mike and Joe were in first and third grades respectively.

I was alone all day for the first time in sixteen years. I liked being alone most of the time, but sometimes I would find that I was worrying about Jess more than made sense. When this happened I would get busy and go visiting or shopping. Jess's health seemed better than ever. I just had too much time on my hands.

At Christmastime we spent some time at the lake. There I became friendly with a woman in the next trailer. She told me about a group that had started in Minneapolis for people with emotional problems. It was a group based on the principles of Alcoholics Anonymous as adapted for emotional problems. I was interested. I didn't show it then, but the twelve steps of Emotions Anonymous were to change my life dramatically.

I went to a meeting in January, then a few more in February. By March 1 I was hooked. I had grasped the "program." It could, indeed, change a person's life-style. I would like to list the twelve steps for you here. If these twelve steps appeal to you, dear reader, I suggest that you contact Emotions Anonymous.*

The Twelve Suggested Steps of Emotions Anonymous

1. We admitted we were powerless over our emotions—that our lives had become unmanageable.
2. Came to believe that a Power greater than ourselves could restore us to sanity.
3. Made a decision to turn our will and our lives over to the care of God—as we understood Him.
4. Made a searching and fearless moral inventory of ourselves.
5. Admitted to God, to ourselves and to another human being the exact nature of our wrongs.
6. Were entirely ready to have God remove all these defects of character.
7. Humbly asked Him to remove our shortcomings.
8. Made a list of all persons we had harmed, and became willing to make amends to them all.
9. Made direct amends to such people wherever possible, except when to do so would injure them or others.

* Emotions Anonymous, P. O. Box 5045, St. Paul, Minnesota 55104

10. Continued to take personal inventory and when we were wrong promptly admitted it.

11. Sought through prayer and meditation to improve our conscious contact with God—as we understood Him, praying only for knowledge of His will for us and the power to carry that out.

12. Having a spiritual awakening as the result of these steps, we tried to carry this message, and to practice these principles in all our affairs.

Taken in one gulp the twelve steps are pretty overwhelming. But taken one step at a time life becomes easier. I began to realize that I was not a god. I saw that most of my nerves and exhaustion were coming from trying too hard to be the perfect wife and mother. I willingly gave up the enormous strain of trying to keep my husband well and my children on the straight and narrow all by myself. I quit seeing myself as the prime mover in our home, and began to learn acceptance. With acceptance I began to regain my physical and emotional strength.

If you don't like this version, here's another version you can try.

The Humorous Twelve Steps

1. I decided I could handle my emotional problems if other people would just quit trying to run my life.

2. I firmly believe that there is no greater power than myself, and anyone who said so was insane.

3. I made a decision to remove my will and my life from God, who didn't understand me anyhow.

4. I made a searching and thorough moral inventory of everyone I know, so they couldn't fool me and take advantage of my good nature.

5. I sought these people out and tried to get them to admit to me, by God, the exact nature of their wrongs.

6. I became willing to help these people get rid of these defects of character.

7. I was humble enough to ask these people to remove their shortcomings.

8. I kept a list of all the people who had harmed me and waited patiently for a chance to get even with them.

9. I got even with these people whenever possible, except when to do so would get me into trouble, too.

10. I continued to take everyone's inventory and when they were wrong, which was most of the time, I promptly made them admit it.

11. Sought through the concentration of my will power to get God, who didn't understand me anyhow, to see that my ideas were best and He ought to give me the power to carry them out.

12. Having maintained my emotional problems for twenty-five years with these steps, I can thoroughly recommend them to others who don't want to lose their hard-earned status, but wish to be left alone to practice neurosis in everything they do for the rest of the days of their lives.

Borrowed from Alcoholics Anonymous
and adapted for Emotions Anonymous
E. A. Messenger, December 1972

In April of 1967 all hell broke loose. I had a hysterectomy. Five days after I returned home, Jess came up from the basement, looked at me, groaned, and collapsed. We took another hectic ride to the hospital. This time he was not to come home until July. One of our daughters buckled under the strain and was hospitalized. A few weeks later a retaining wall collapsed, pinning seven-year-old Mike by the leg. His leg was broken and badly bowed. I now had three of the seven members of our family in three different hospitals, and here I had been planning a nice easy recovery from my own surgery.

Acceptance. Acceptance. It was hard to accept our problems, but with gritted teeth I plowed through each day. Now, with hindsight, I can see that when one thing goes wrong in a family, everyone else in that family is set up for accidents and illness. We were all off our feed. So the inevitable happened, and catastrophe followed catastrophe.

At the time I had all I could do to travel from one hospital to another, comforting, delivering messages of progress from one victim to another, and racing back home to join the three well children for a thrown-together supper. I hated being in the house at night without Jess. I wasn't without another adult for long. Word of our circumstances traveled around campus rapidly. Soon, the girls from Clovia sorority, a college 4-H sorority, arrived at my door. These girls knew and loved Jess (he was their adviser for two years). From the first of May until early July I was never alone with the children again. When Mike came home from the hospital with a cast from the top of his leg to the tip of his toes, some fraternity boys gave him daily rides to and from school. There is no way I can ever repay those young people. How truly wonderful they were.

We still hear from some of them even now. They are all married and have children. How rapidly the years go by.

9

Jess

My heart is a funny thing. Hearts are supposed to be pumps, nice machines that keep working smoothly no matter what. But my pump isn't like that. It has feelings. It is sensitive to what I'm doing. When I was happy and relaxed I never had any heart pain or angina. Even when I was doing something fairly strenuous like walking through the marsh deer hunting I wouldn't get angina. Granted, I was going easily and I never did things like trying to drag a deer.

But the next week I could be walking the five blocks to school, hurrying a little and walking uphill slightly, and right away I would get a little chest pain. My heart was telling me it was working in a way it didn't like. So now I had an indicator to tell me when I was doing the least little thing more than I should.

The only trouble with my indicator was that it scared hell out of me.

Before my heart attack I had nothing to tell me I was overdoing and I would go way past my limit until I would

144

get a three-day sinus attack or get sick some other way. Or, I would get depressed.

When I was in my own business I would have periods where I would get so depressed that I would be paralyzed by it. I would go to my office with important things to do and I would be completely unable to do them.

I would end up wandering around town going into stores and buying things or going to the library and reading hunting books. It was a good thing I didn't care for bars or I would have been an alcoholic. The knowledge that my work was undone couldn't bring me out of it.

Each day the depression went on my problems would grow worse because deadlines were getting closer and closer. The consequences of putting things off would grow more and more serious. Sometimes those depressions would last for a week.

I can see now that those sinus attacks and week-long depressions were my body's way of resting itself. They were the price I paid then for forcing myself to work too hard and too long at work I didn't believe in and at what I thought was recreation but was just overdriven activity.

I don't remember how many times I was in the hospital in my first five years after my heart attack. I would guess four or five. But I have a happy ability to forget many of the unpleasant things that happen, so it could have been more times than that.

Going to the hospital was bad, but even worse was my fear. I remember a story in a book I read after my heart attack. A writer who had had a heart attack wrote a book, I think called *Episode,* in which he told of his fear. He was constantly taking his own pulse to see if his heart was still beating. One day he had lunch with his doctor, who remarked, "I can see that you are lots better. We have gone all through this lunch hour without you taking your pulse."

I laughed at that man's story. I thought his fear was pathetic. I can see now that I was even more afraid than he was. I was so afraid that I couldn't even admit it to myself.

In the old story about the sword of Damocles, a sword is hanging by a single hair over a man's head. At any second it can come crashing down and kill the man. That is how I felt. Inside my chest was a heart that any second could stop. When I had pain, my heart seemed to be saying very loudly, "This might be your very last minute on earth."

I know we need to face our death. My heart attack made me face death as something real and close in. But I don't think we can stand the constant awareness of the threat of our own death.

When I found that I would have to have heart surgery, I went back to the farm to see Bits. By now I was forty and Bits was about thirty-five. I told him I was going in for surgery and that I was a little apprehensive.

Bits was squatting on the ground working on a piece of farm machinery. He just looked up and said, "Hell, Jess, there ain't a one of us going to get out of this thing alive."

I don't know why, but that hurt me. I guess I wanted him to tell me that death would never come to us. But not Bits. He had a fine acceptance of life and death, which are just two sides of the same coin.

I was struck recently by a strange thing about Elizabeth Kubler-Ross's research on death. She asked a friend to send me her book on dying. In studying the five steps she found patients went through in accepting their death, I saw the steps were very similar to the ones I saw myself and others go through in accepting life: denial, anger, bargaining, depression, and acceptance.

There is a line in the book *Little Big Man* where our hero wakes up in Lodge Skins's tepee after being saved from death at Little Bighorn. Little Big Man realizes he isn't dead. And he said about himself, "Once you should of died and didn't, you ain't ever the same."

Having faced death a few times, I thought he meant

that statement in a good way. I thought he meant once you have faced death you appreciate life more. In a way this is so. I recently saw a statement to the effect that each of us needs to stop our denial of death long enough to see it as something that can happen to us so we live today instead of always tomorrow or yesterday. But then, this statement said, we need to pick up our denial of death again and go on denying it until the end.

I believe that. I think that because I was faced with death so squarely and so frighteningly, too many of my defenses against death were stripped away. And my frequent angina made it too hard for me to pick up any denial of my death so I could live life without so much fear.

The saying "Live each day as if it were the last" is true. But we need a balance to that.

There is a story about an old Greek man who was going to plant trees outside the village. The kids were throwing rocks at him and taunting him. "Old man, you will never live to see those trees grow. Why do you plant them?" To this the old man replied, "I live each day as if I would live to be a thousand." That is the knowledge I need to get into my heart. It is in my head but I need it in my heart.

In one of the stories in the book *Wyeth People* an old character talks about planting trees even though he is too old to see them grow big. He says, "If a thing is a good thing to do, it doesn't ever stop being a good thing."

In the five years after my heart attack my fear was a big problem to me. The constant warnings I got from my heart and my body told me I didn't have much reserve and that I was too often very close to the edge. With those frequent signals, it was harder to handle my fear, too; my fear made me do many frantic things and it made it hard for me to get much serenity.

So when I heard I should consider the new heart surgery that was available I was partly relieved.

Men with angina so bad they couldn't be active at all

were playing golf a year later and working normally. One man with a bad heart was able to go back to work at the newspaper loading bundles of papers into the trucks.

I had gone to the hospital in April with some heart symptoms. They sent me home for a few days to rest up, then brought me back in for the test of my heart.

The test is frightening but tremendously valuable. A special dye is injected into the heart arteries. As the dye moves through the arteries motion picture X rays are taken. These show exactly the condition of those arteries. The spots where arteries narrow dangerously is clear. A clot or blockage in an old artery where a heart attack occurred shows up along with the new pathways around the blockage that developed after the heart attack.

My test showed that my arteries may have been small to start with, which could have been inherited. But they were also blocked some, so that the lower corner of the heart wasn't getting as much blood as it needed. I could benefit from the surgery.

The surgery I had five years ago used the two internal mammary arteries that feed the chest area with blood. These two arteries can be spared their primary function so are disconnected and hooked up to the heart. On me they were hooked into the heart in the lower corner in both the front and back sides. Small cuts were made in the heart muscle and the arteries were carried into tunnels. Branches from these arteries developed connections with the coronary artery system deeper in the heart muscle. It would take six months to a year for the maximum amount of blood to get through by these new connections.

The big advantages were that my heart would have an additional blood supply where it was needed the most and the new arteries would bring a new blood supply into the heart to areas where a heart attack would most likely occur. If I did have another blockage in a heart artery, new blood would be coming in below the block to help make the blockage less serious.

After the tests, they kept me in the hospital instead of sending me home as they did most heart patients. I don't know if it was because my arteries were so bad or because I was such a wild man, or both. Anyway, I had to wait there two or three weeks for my surgery.

That was a strange time. I was feeling fine but I had to stay in the hospital. I knew what was coming so it was hard being very calm.

Fortunately, I had an enjoyable roommate again. Most of the time before surgery, my roommate was Tom. He was a handsome young guy about twenty-five and built like a Greek god. With him in the room, we both got lots of nursing attention. All Tom had wrong with him was a minor question on his plumbing so he was in good spirits. We stole chairs out of most of the rooms of the sick people who didn't need them so we could have chairs for our nurses and our friends.

There were lots of student nurses on that floor and they made our room their coffee place. Tom and I ordered lots of chocolate milks and ice creams, then saved them in the refrigerator to make chocolate milk shakes in the evening for our nurses when the shifts changed.

I liked to drink hard cider so my friends brought quarts or half gallons when they came to visit. We saved our juice glasses each day until we had about twenty glasses for our bar. Some of our guests drank more than they brought but it usually evened out. A couple of times I ran low on cider. One time I called a teetotaling friend and had him make a stop at the liquor store for me. Another time the liquor store made a delivery to my room at St. Mary's Hospital in Minneapolis.

We had an old nun who was in charge of praying on our floor—Sister Ethel. She was really strong-minded.

She kept scolding me because I would open the window when our room got hot. She claimed it fouled up the air conditioning. I claimed the air conditioning must not work very well because our room was so hot. She insisted rules were rules and the windows must be closed.

"Okay, Sister," I told her, "I will close the windows when you are in our room, but when you leave I will open them again if it is hot. Remember, Sister, I'm an old Baptist, so you don't scare me."

Sister Ethel always wanted to pray for me. That was fine with me because I needed it. When she wanted me to have the last rites of the Church before my surgery I thought that was fine too, but I had had the last rites about five times already and my wife was embarrassed about me having them again. I told Sister Ethel this and she said she understood.

A few days later she said, "Could I have Father McDonough say a few prayers over you?" I said, "Okay, just as long as it isn't the last rites." Sister Ethel said, "No, these are different prayers than those you had."

Father McDonough came in that night and said the last rites for me again. That was fine with me because the more prayers, the better.

The next day I asked Sister Ethel why she told me such a big lie. She said, "I didn't lie to you. Those were different prayers than were said over you before. Those were the last rites said in English. Before they were in Latin."

As you can plainly see, I carried my coronary personality right into the hospital with me. My only progress was that I didn't get things as screwed up in that room as I had when I was in the hospital with my heart attack five years earlier.

The days went by very well and my fear didn't get too bad except sometimes in the early mornings when I would wake up and no one was around.

There was a nurse on the night shift who made those times much easier just because she was there. I didn't even come to know her name. Each morning she would come in my room early just before she went off duty. She would put her hand on my shoulder and say, "Good morning, Mr. Lair." But there was something about her that was so calming to me that I felt better immediately. There was so much woman reflected in just her greeting and light touch.

The night before the surgery was a bad night. I was very frightened and I was too dumb to ask for tranquilizers. My surgery had been fitted in on top of another operation so I was going to have to wait until early afternoon before I went to surgery. When the fear would come that night I would pray the best I could and go to sleep. The last time I woke during the night it was about four o'clock. All of a sudden I saw myself going through the surgery all right and I felt a deep calm—a serenity that was such a marked contrast to my wild activity of the past two or three weeks.

Thank God for that serenity. I sure needed it that morning. They forgot to give me a hypo before surgery. So I sat through the morning of waiting with Jackie without any sedation and went down to surgery wide-eyed. The nurse came in about noon to wheel me down to surgery. Sister Ethel walked alongside the cart pinning holy medals on me. The nurse wheeled my cart up to the door of the surgery suite and then turned and walked away. I suppose she had something important to do. I sure hope so because I know I needed her bad just then. I had twenty minutes to a half hour of waiting there for the nurses from surgery to come and get me. I know it was a long wait because I could see a clock through a window.

That experience has always been a lesson to me to try to pay attention to the people around me so I can see when they might need me. I know I can't always see their need. And even when I see it I can't always do anything about it. But because of that experience I try to look a lot harder now.

When I finally was wheeled into the operating room, the nurses were pleasant and reassuring. In a few minutes they started the anesthesia. I woke up in the recovery room all wrung out and numb. The first person I was conscious of was Jackie. I told her, "Don't worry about me, honey, I'm over the hill." I still had the serenity that came to me early that morning. I needed it for the pain ahead.

I didn't have to see myself so I was spared the worst horror of how I looked. But I had to lie there with all those wires and tubes coming out of me, listening to the machine that sounded at every heartbeat and watching the scope that monitored my EKG.

Please don't misunderstand me. I don't want to scare off anyone who needs surgery. The opposite is the case. I'm trying to get my friends to have the test and surgery if they need it. If I need it, I'll go back through it again because hard as that pain is it beats hell out of the alternative, which is the fear you have to live with lacking the benefits of the surgery.

In a few days that pain is over. Men, women, and children take pain like that every day. I can, too.

There was a nurse in intensive care who was the greatest nurse I've ever seen or heard of. The first full day in intensive care she was off duty. A different nurse took care of me that day. She tried to give me a bath and then handed me the washcloth so I could finish my bath. Sorry, but I didn't have the strength.

The next day Gladys was on duty. She bustled around the place hollering at us for not coughing to clear our lungs. She would lift up our chests to make it easier for us to cough.

When it came time to give me a bath she cheerily started in at the top and moved steadily to the bottom.

She wasn't squeamish and she knew my privacy wasn't very important to me in the shape I was in.

The intensive care unit I was in had five beds. The first full day I was there, three of them were occupied. There was a little baby a few feet to the right of me who had just had surgery to correct a heart defect. The baby was fighting for his life.

Across the room from me was a guy a few years younger than me who had had the same surgery I had. He was operated on in the morning, came in in the early afternoon, and was in trouble by evening. They couldn't get him to cough. When they finally did, they found he was bleeding internally from a small artery that was leaking. So they rushed him back to surgery to solve his problem.

The second day they were again fighting hard to save the little baby. He developed a stress ulcer from the surgery and was bleeding. At times, ten to fifteen doctors and nurses with their equipment were crowded around his bed. I was starting to be conscious enough to realize what was going on. My heartbeat kept steadily beeping along until about that afternoon, I think it was, when all of a sudden it beat fast and irregularly. I called Gladys over right away and she immediately got some medicine for my arrhythmia. In an hour or so the beat was normal again.

The next day I was more conscious and the little baby was worse. There was a big crowd around his bed and I couldn't take it any more. I called Gladys over and told her. I don't recall her waiting for instructions or anything. She called a couple of nurses to help her. They loaded all my gear on the bed and moved me into an adjoining room with glass windows looking into the main intensive care room. Then she moved Don Logelin (the one with heart surgery like mine), in with me, so it was the two of us together.

Don and I had hollered some remarks back and forth at each other in the big intensive care room. But now we were closer together and where we wouldn't disturb anyone. Don went to work to make me feel good. He kidded everyone and everything to do with our care. As near as I can see, he was God-sent to heal me. In our sixth day we went into regular rooms to stay six more days before we would go home.

A few days after we were out of intensive care, Don and I heard a woman scream. It sounded as though it was down the hall in the waiting room. My first thought was that it was the baby's mother and that he had died. He had.

The scream was partly because one of the nurses in intensive care, a big rough woman, very coldly told the mother her baby was dead. I know there is no good way. But this woman had been rough, even cruel, to both Don and I. Her hardness was probably her defense against the terror and death so common in intensive care. But she added to the grief in that room and was soon removed.

There were three other heart surgery patients who had been in intensive care with Don and I. They had had different operations than we had. One of the three, a woman, seemed doomed from the start. She didn't seem to want to live. Don and I were so conscious of that because we both wanted to live badly. She died. The baby died. And the third person died. So Don and I were the only two of the five of us united by coincidence who were alive ten days later. That frightened me.

I don't know why I responded so well and so fast to the surgery. I guess you aren't supposed to get much new blood into your heart right away. But I felt a world better, even with the lingering pain and weakness from the surgery. I suppose the benefit was psychological, but I sure benefited.

Since my surgery, they have developed another method. They take a piece of vein out of the leg and use it to bypass the bad area in the heart. The vein is hooked right into the heart's system of arteries so there is an immediate positive effect. The surgery gives such a strong, quick effect that it is even being used on heart attack victims during the first few days after their heart attacks.

During all the time I was in the hospital Jackie was going through hell. Two others in the family were in the hospital. She had some terrible family problems she had to go through alone. At the time before my surgery she had to walk into the hospital every day as if nothing had happened. Then, when she got to the hospital, she would find, not her husband, but a fear-crazed coronary idiot who was grasping at anything to keep himself barely afloat as he waited for surgery.

This has been one of the unbelievable things to me about my wife. I married a nineteen-year-old gorgeous doll who was a beautiful listener and ended up with a woman who was solid steel when she had to be. She reminds me of one of my favorite sayings, "She has the strength of ten because her heart is pure." In her case it is true. If it hadn't been, she couldn't have helped lead us all through our hell; and so often, it seems, our life is having hell for breakfast.

So Jackie got all of us through our hospital stays, got me home, packed up the house, rented it out, and got ready to move to Montana—all by herself.

I had spent twenty-five years in Minneapolis and St. Paul. I had gone to high school and college there. I had worked at many jobs, had my own business, and been very active in many kinds of organizations. Yet in all that time my bones had never been comfortable in the Twin Cities. As I would drive on the freeways I kept looking at guys, wondering where they worked, who they were, how much money they made, were they doing better than me. It was insane to feel that way but feelings don't have any heads, they are just feelings. So I was going to go to Montana to see if that was a place where my bones would feel comfortable. In case it wasn't, we had protected ourselves because we had just taken a year's leave of absence and rented the house.

Jackie drove us to Montana in two days. I sat opposite her. I was weak, skinny, excited, and worried some.

10

Jackie

Heart surgery! Progress had been made on the operation Jess's doctor had mentioned so many months ago. When we met our first heart specialist, we found that by coincidence the leading heart specialist and the leading heart surgeon at St. Mary's Hospital were both Italians. Both men have the warm, friendly love of people that is a virtue of so many southern Europeans. These doctors were good for us.

How did I feel about heart surgery? From my standpoint it was a welcome suggestion. The particular surgery available then (a double internal mammary implant) was fairly new, but results were good. The unused mammary arteries were taken from the inside of the chest and implanted into the section of the heart where most heart attacks occur. This offered a fresh new blood supply to the chest.

It sounded simple and logical. First the doctors wanted to see Jess's heart and arteries more clearly. They ordered a heart catheterization. This involves opening a vein in the bend of the arm and running a small catheter into it. The catheter is run up the arm to the chest and down the chest to the heart. It made me sick just to think of it. Jess took the test well. I thought the test seemed worse than any surgery I knew of.

As I write this now, five and one half years later, I must tell you what I am going through. Jess and I write in our camping trailer, which is parked at the side of the garage. I walked outside this warm morning in August with a hot cup of tea in my hand. I am cold. My head aches. I have a backache and pains in my chest. I sit in the trailer and grouse at Jess. I get up and slam out the door. Back in the house I decide I am hungry. I start to fix some eggs. Good God, I am crying. Why? I know. I don't want to think about the heart surgery days. But I have to. The hell I do. The book can go to hell. God, I'm cold. I'll put on my ski jacket, then I'll take another hot cup of tea and get out there and write about it. It's like having a baby. It hurts for a while, but when it's over, it's over.

Jess stayed in the hospital, except for a day's leave home here and there, until his surgery in June. The day of his surgery he was scheduled to go up at noon. I arrived at St. Mary's early that morning. Jess was tense, but talking very peacefully. He didn't fool me. I crawled into bed with him and held him, to hell with hospital rules. I am a compulsive rule keeper, but that day I found the strength to break one. Jess relaxed a little. Relatives came in to say hello and good luck. My mother came to say hello and to wait with me. I resented them all. I wanted to be alone with Jess. Noon arrived. The cart came. Jess hopped out of bed and onto the cart. Two attendants wheeled him off. I broke into a million splinters inside. I wanted to snatch him and take him home. He didn't know this. My outside smiled and patted him and said, "Goodbye, I'll see you later." I went down to the third-floor surgical waiting room.

I don't remember the next hours at all. Family came and went. I paced the floor. I looked outside at the traffic whizzing by. My mother went home to be with our children. They needed her more than I did, and they all truly loved Grandma Bim.

About five o'clock, the heart surgeon walked into the waiting room and told me Jess had come through surgery fine and was in the heart intensive care room. "All we have to worry about now is hemorrhage or arrhythmia. If these don't happen, he'll be as good as new." I knew what hemorrhage was. I guessed that arrhythmia was something wrong with his heartbeat—I was close enough. A few seconds after the doctor left, a nurse came and told me I could peek at him.

Ginny, the nurse, was a woman we had known in one of our old neighborhoods. It was nice to see a familiar face. I walked into the corridor with her through doors marked "Intensive Care. Visiting Hours: five minutes every two hours." Jess was in a private room on the left, with windows looking out on the nurse's desk. Nothing in the world could have prepared me for the first glimpse of my husband.

Ginny told me he would be asleep. He wouldn't know I was there. I stepped just inside the door. My God, that couldn't be Jess. I truly did not know that thing on the bed. His chest was naked except for a thin strip of tape covering the incision. Out of his chest came three tubes with rubber hoses attached. There were electrodes fastened here and there. They ran to a continuous EKG machine that went "squeak, squeak, squeak."

Jess stirred and a giant test tube at the bottom of the bed went splat! It was blood from his chest running into the tube. There were assorted other machinery around the bed making odd noises and little lights flickering on and off. There were some bottles of solution hanging around the bed and running into his arm and leg. One was blood, the other intravenous solution. There was the hiss of oxygen running into a face mask on that stranger. But that was no stranger, that was Jess. Just then my husband, who wasn't supposed to know I was there, turned his head, pulled down his oxygen mask with the hand that wasn't taped to a board, opened his startling blue eyes, and said, "Hi, Jac, I'm going to make it."

That was too much for me. I went out in the hall with everything turning black around me. Ginny grabbed my head and pushed it down toward my knees. I slid down the wall and sat on the floor. I wanted to faint. I wanted to run; I had seen all that I could stand for one day. I got up, apologized for my behavior, and ran for the waiting room. I was hot one minute, cold the next, nauseated the next. I went into the bathroom and threw up, then crumpled into a chair in the waiting room.

I couldn't understand what was the matter with me. The surgery was over. I just wasn't prepared for all of that foreign-looking machinery. I had to get hold of myself. Jess was, after all, alive. But he was so blue. I wondered why I had to see him so soon. I wept inside, and sat frozen outside.

In a little while the panic calmed and I reached for a cigarette. We were going to make it. Things were a little sloppy there for a minute, but I was able to take a deep breath. Life does go on. I called the children. I told them Dad was fine. I said that I would be home sometime tomorrow. Ginny brought me a pillow and blanket. I slept fitfully for a few hours.

I realized that nothing the doctors might have told me could prepare me for the fact.

The heart is an emotional as well as a physical thing. Until only recent times, heartbeat and blood pressure readings were used as the final diagnosis of life or death.

There are many supercharged beliefs and superstitions centering around the heart. One has tonsils removed or gall bladder surgery and this is taken as a matter of course. But say "heart surgery" and everyone reacts as though stung with a cattle prod.

To the family awaiting the results of heart surgery this is especially true. Along with the very real trauma involved come the superstitions and fears of generations.

I think there is no escaping this. One must try to get through the days as best one can. There are no magic formulas or easy ways. I am trying to tell the bare bones of how I felt and reacted in the hope that the reader can see that if I survived the trauma, so can he if called upon.

The next few days were hard. The anesthetic had worn off and Jess was in pain. He had been moved early that morning into a large bed ward on the other side of the nurse's desk. Beside his bed was a baby bed. A tiny baby who had had heart surgery was mewing like a newborn kitten. The two beds across the aisle were empty. One of them was occupied later that morning by Don Logelin, who at that moment was having the same heart surgery as Jess.

The nurses were later going to dub Jess and Don "the Gold Dust Twins."

In the meantime Jess was in agony. He wanted me to rub the right side of his chest. He was restless and drugged. Minutes seemed like hours to him. Hours seemed like days. Every twenty minutes or so he would yell for a hypo. He got one every two hours at first, but they didn't seem to be doing much good as far as I could see. Later I realized that Jess never did remember that first day very well, so all of his groaning and muttering wasn't as meaningful as I thought.

Marlys Pritchard arrived from Clearwater Lake. The nurses let us be with Jess quite a bit. I would rub his chest until my arm ached and then Marlys would slip her hand under mine and rub without a break in the rhythm.

The morning passed.

Don Logelin arrived. We were asked to step outside.

We went down to the waiting room and I met Don's wife, Arlene. We became close companions in our shared misery. Soon a nurse came and told Arlene she could go and see Don. Don's brother went down with her. Arlene peeked and came away. Don's brother fell in the hall. I wasn't such a coward after all, if that huge man fainted. I felt better about the night before.

A little while later I returned to the "heart room," as we had dubbed that particular intensive care ward. Jess was still demanding that his chest be rubbed. Gladys Mienz, a nurse who would follow our Gold Dust Twins through their entire hospitalization, nodded that I could begin to rub again. Marlys had left, so I rubbed on by myself.

Across the aisle Don was having a hard time. Nurses and doctors were bending over the bed. The nurses kept saying, "Take a deep breath, Don. Breathe, Breathe." Don sounded awful. He finally yelled, very loudly for a sick man, "If I have to keep breathing to live then I'm dead." There was quick movement around his bed. The whole bed was suddenly moving out the door with a nurse riding it sitting on one leg. There was no time to ask me to step outside. Don was hemorrhaging. He went through the surgery doors rapidly. I felt faint and sick again.

I left Jess and went back to the waiting room to sit down. Alrene was white and frightened. She already knew Don was back in surgery. I was glad I didn't have to tell her. I couldn't have. I didn't know what to say.

We waited for what seemed like a long time. Don returned to the heart room. He was quiet now. He was going to make it, too. I decided it was time to leave. I hadn't seen the children for thirty-six hours.

On Dudley Avenue everyone was sitting on the front porch. Barbara was strumming her guitar and singing in her sweet, clear voice. Barb and I harmonized on "Edelweiss." Grandma Bim sat there with tears running down her face. It had been a hard time for all of us.

I tossed and turned in our bed, expecting the phone to ring all night long. In the morning I was terribly torn between being with the children and going back to the hospital. I realized there was no peace at either place, but I felt better at the hospital and I knew Bim had things in order at home. I returned to St. Mary's.

Jess was quieter today. Don was quiet. The tiny baby next to Jess was in trouble. I couldn't look. The young parents of the weak babe were in a separate room reserved for the families of the critically ill. I felt sympathy for them, but I did not have the energy to become involved in their agony.

The day passed and I went home to another restless night. When I returned to St. Mary's the next morning the Gold Dust Twins had been moved from the heart room into a double room down the hall. The baby was dying and Jess was awake enough to be bothered by the awful truth. Gladys listened to Jess's fears about the baby and it was decided that Jess and Don were far enough along to be moved.

This was progress. I relaxed a little more. They were still in intensive care but they were two doors removed from the nurse's station. The blood transfusions were gone. Jess's I.V. was gone; Don still had a day to go before that needle was removed. The men were still hooked up to that infernal machinery, but I was accustomed to it now and it didn't frighten me. And I had company in Don's wife. We had lunch together and traded off hours to see our husbands. The nurses had tightened up the schedule again and we were only allowed five minutes every two hours. Another good sign that things were looking up.

I have gone into fairly great detail here, not because I want to be ghoulish, but because heart surgery is becoming a commonplace. Many of us will share this ordeal; some surgeries are more dangerous than others, but all of them traumatic to the whole family.

Someday perhaps we will think little of having our hearts operated on, but for the present, I am sure you join me in still being somewhat aghast at these procedures.

At home, I had another problem. Before he got sick Jess had accepted a job at the English Department at Montana State University. He had taken a year's leave of absence from the University of Minnesota. Just before heart surgery he had agreed we had no choice but to move to Montana, for Jess's job at the St. Paul campus had been filled. We decided not to let people in Bozeman know that he was ill: We would put our faith in God and the doctors to make him well enough to move. I received a call from Dr. Parker of the English Department at Bozeman. He wanted to know what textbooks Jess wanted to use that fall. I lied and told him Jess was out of town. I said I would ask Jess and that Jess would write and tell him.

We had placed an ad in the Bozeman *Chronicle* for a house. A letter came telling about a house on South Bozeman with four bedrooms. I wrote the owner and said we would take it, sight unseen. The lease arrived, I signed for both Jess and me. I wrote a letter to John Parker telling him what texts Jess wanted. I again signed Jess's name. Our secret was still safe. But it troubled me to lie. What choice did we have, though? Jess no longer had a job at Minnesota, we had five children to feed. We were going to Montana by hook or by crook. Besides, school didn't start until the middle of September. This was the middle of June. Jess had three months to recuperate. If I had told the people in Montana that he had had heart surgery, I would have frightened them to death. I still think we took the only course of action open to us.

The weeks sped by and on July 5 Jess came home.

For the first time in almost three months we had Dad home with us. We could take anything as long as we were together. Jess never was one to stay in bed very long. In a few days he was up most of the day. He sat in his big leather recliner in the living room. He and I walked around in the yard at first, then over to the neighbors. Soon it was a walk to the corner, then around the block.

A few weeks after he came home we ventured up to Clearwater Lake for a last weekend in our trailer. We had sold it in preparation for our move to Montana.

Don and Arlene Logelin were staying in their cabin just a few miles south of us. We drove over for the afternoon.

I thought Jess was active! Don was running around as though he had never been sick at all. The men compared scars and we parted fondly. Don and Arlene said they would be out to see us in Montana. They planned a trip out west in August.

I sometimes think we were all crazy. But the fact remains that Jess and Don progressed faster with fewer problems than any of the other "hearts." Perhaps there was sense in our gung-ho attitude after all.

The last week of July arrived. Our last week in our home. Jess went down to the basement to pack HIS junk. His junk was in a workroom. It was junk to me, but precious to him. He was making his own split bamboo fly rod on a form that was made by Whit Longstaff and Starke Hathaway, both psychologists at the University of Minnesota. Dr. Longstaff had given his precious bamboo brought out of Tonkin, Indochina, before World War II, to Jess before he died. Dr. Hathaway gave Jess the form he and Whit had used. Jess spent hours and hours whittling bamboo and fingertips, both before and after his surgery. Jess had many of his father's carpenter tools. He had guns, and fishing equipment, duck decoys, boxes of old leather, bags of old metal, tins of nails and screws. His junk weighed as much as the furniture in our house. It was all packed. Our tons of books were boxed. Moving day was here.

I hated to leave Minneapolis and the doctors. I needed the security of my setting, but my setting was being loaded onto the biggest moving van I had ever seen in my life.

I felt lonely and frightened, but sensed a need to keep my feelings from Jess and the children.

From deep inside a feeling was growing. I guess I was finally growing up. I felt then and still feel today, that the major source of peace and security for my children and my husband *must* be me. I began to put aside my childish neuroses. I found strength from that feeling, from that knowledge that I was the "well" one. I began to realize that the root of these neuroses was truly in my mind instead of my body.

I slipped a few times in the first few years in Bozeman, but I have had a steady growth in strength both mental and physical since those first few days after Jess's heart surgery. There is a quote attributed to Ted Kennedy that I keep beside me. I don't even know where it came from, but it has been a comfort to me.

"There are those of us who may always have to live lives forever dedicated by a force we shall never understand, but so long as we remain steadfast enough to emerge from our personal trials stronger within ourselves and more compassionate to those around us, it will, I feel sure, all be worth the pain and suffering we or our loved ones endure . . ."

The last of the furniture was loaded. It was nightfall. The van driver walked up to me. "We'll see you in Bozeman day after tomorrow." He left.

I was frightened. The doctors had recommended a three-day trip for Jess. We were only to drive about 350 miles per day. We had no choice. We had to be in Bozeman in two days. That meant two long days of 500 miles per day. I had to do all of the driving by myself. Jess could not drive yet, and none of the children were old enough to drive.

We would do it. I had the "strength of ten." We piled into the station wagon. We had a mattress and pillows in the back for Jess and the children to take turns resting on. The kitten found a place in Joe's lap and went to sleep. We drove to the western edge of Minneapolis and spent the night of July 31 with friends.

Tomorrow morning we would head west toward Montana and a new life.

11

Jess

I was a dumb Norwegian flatlander who came from Minnesota to Montana wearing a cowboy suit. I was living a childish part of me. But I was living a part of me that I had never let live much before in my forty years. I had always been so preoccupied with growing up and being a big success. I had always been so concerned about what other people thought of me that there was no room for the me that God made to come into the picture.

So there was a lot of little boy in me. Why shouldn't there have been? I had never taken the time to let the little boy have his day. But now my wife and children and the people around me were willing to let the little boy come out and were willing to be patient and let him grow up. But most importantly, I myself was finally becoming more willing to let the childish behavior out and I was better able to stand it when I saw it.

It's not easy for a supposedly grown man who consorts with other grown men of affairs and who reads books about men like Thomas Jefferson building Monticello before he was forty and yet who has to see himself putting on the "cowboy suit his mommy bought him." But I was sustained when I came to Montana as I am now, by my question at the time of my heart attack: "Is this something I believe in?" I had to answer that it was. And while I could see how childish what I was doing was, I was supported by the love and the belief given me by my family and a few other people who had loved me.

When we pulled into Bozeman, we asked directions at a gas station to the house Jackie had rented sight unseen. One of the guys who worked there was Kenny Graber, a hunting guide. He responded to my interest in the mountains and hunting by offering to take me riding. Two months after my heart surgery, I made a fifteen-mile horseback ride to Deer Lake in the Gallatin Canyon, where Kenny was putting in a sheep hunting camp. It was my first taste of one of the things I had come to Montana for.

When I first drove down the Gallatin Canyon to Bozeman three years earlier, I kept looking at the high hills along the road and wondered what was on the other side of them. Now I knew what was behind one particular range of hills. I used to have the same questions continually in my mind as I drove through Montana on vacations: What kind of country is back in there? What does it look like? How does it feel to be in there? Where does that little road lead to? What's it like on the other side of the mountain?

Soon after I came to Montana, I bought a small green jeep for $350. With my sons I started off up the mountain roads exploring the country. The jeep kept breaking down and needed little things like a new engine or a rebuilt front end. After about a thousand dollars' worth of repairs, I had a pretty good jeep.

I started buying maps of the mountains and began planning my hunting trips. I hadn't lived in the state six months, so I had to pay $100 for a non-resident license.

The fall after my heart surgery I was in the mountains hunting deer and elk with my jeep. But I knew so little about hunting in the West that I could just as well have been hunting in my back yard for all the chance I had doing what I was doing.

This, then, was the pace of my recreation when I came here. I had always been driven to overdo. The five years of my heart attack had placed a limit on my physical overdoing, but it hadn't slowed my mind down. So I was driven in my head when I was sitting still. Now I didn't have my heart pain to hold me back, so I could, within reason, do many of the things I wanted to do.

This thing I see in myself I also see in so many of the coronary types. We can't seem to enjoy a little of anything. We have to have great gulps. We are like men who think they face starvation and so shovel food in their mouths with both hands.

This type of frantic activity can barely be handled by a man as healthy as a horse. If, like me, there is a bodily disposition to heart trouble, the coronary type eventually pays the price with a heart attack. But the heart attack is less significant than that wild, driven activity. I think it is harmful to a person, no matter how strong he is.

When I go so fast and greedily through life, I hurt myself and the people around me and I don't even see it. I am like a tightrope walker crossing the Niagara Falls gorge. All of us are trying to stay on the rope. But my way of keeping my balance is to jump, twist, and dance on the rope. I may claim it necessary to keep my balance. But I set the tightrope to moving so violently that I knock off the people behind me and ahead of me. And I don't even notice because I am so preoccupied with my own gyrations.

I see my driven activities as a very poor substitute for some more satisfying way of life. But until I find that better game, that more satisfying way, I will stay with the only game I know, no matter how sick and destructive it might be to me and the people around me.

I see heart attacks as coming from a heart that is slowly shriveling up from a lack of love. The physical activities that precipitate the attack are more a symptom of the problem than the problem itself. But most doctors can do so little about feelings and are so afraid of feelings themselves that they concentrate on the patient's physical symptoms and activity.

What I was doing was trying to get to the core of the problem. How could I get some real nourishment for my heart? How could I build some enriching relationships? Well, obviously, there was no way people could love the big fake I was trying to be. How could any human love a mess like that? So I began to search for myself and my way.

It seems like over and over in my life I have to learn this lesson of believing in myself and my way. But constantly I cave in to society and some nebulous "others" whom I can't name. I feel so sure I have to try to please them. Yet there is no way I can please someone else. When I do what *I* believe in, I pretty generally please my God, my family, and many of the people around me.

Over and over I have to learn this same lesson only to find later I haven't learned it well enough. Just recently I was reading the program of a behavior modification conference in California. The stories on the speakers' backgrounds were lengthy and packed with impressive academic achievements and honors. I found myself getting upset that I had done so little with training similar to theirs. I caught myself sinking into the trap of trying to be something I'm not in a vain attempt to impress others.

I'm sad that ten years after my heart attack there is still so much of me that wants to please and impress others at any price. I can't blame society for this. Some of the people in society want me to be me as I am. Yet the egomaniac in me ignores this and wants to please everybody even though I know it is impossible and I would hate myself for doing it. So goes the struggle.

When we came to Bozeman, my wife organized a chapter of Emotions Anonymous. We met some fine Alcoholics Anonymous people who helped us get started by telling their stories. It was good to have the emotional closeness that's available to alcoholics in the AA chapters found in any good-sized town in the United States.

The house we rented cost $185 a month. After we had lived there four months, a neighbor woman came over to the house one afternoon. She was complaining that if she just had $100 more income a month everything would be fine. I was exasperated with her. I thought, "If $100 a month is that crucial, why don't you live in a less expensive neighborhood?"

I didn't say anything to her, but after she left I told Jackie we were going to buy a house cheap enough that we could afford it on the $12,000 I was earning. The next day we started looking at houses. We looked at some dumps that were so dirty and run-down they made me sick to my stomach. But Jackie was brave and didn't show any of the distress she must have felt.

Finally we found a house that would do. The boys would have to sleep in old rooms in the basement with holes in the walls. We put in a bid of $17,000. which was $2,000 less than the asking price. I hoped we wouldn't get the house.

The house had the advantage of being within walking distance from three different schools and my job at the university, so it would cut car expenses and spare Jackie all the work of ferrying kids. But the house was just a common little house. Two doors away was a corner house that was in the process of being destroyed by a group of college football players who lived there. The front yard was a mess and the back yard had some mattresses lying in it in case someone needed a mattress in a hurry.

I was horrified at what my rich and fancy relative might think of me if he came to see me at that house. But it was an unreal and even funny fear, because he has never come to see me and never will.

Our bid and $500 earnest money was accepted. For the next few nights I had nightmares about being associated with that awful house. To me that house was me. It said I was shabby and second-rate. So again, I was wrestling with my foolish concern about appearances. Keep up the appearances. To hell with the cost to your family or your heart. Put up a big front, a big ego scene.

Some friends from Emotions Anonymous and Alcoholics Anonymous helped us get the house ready and we worked hard at making it a warm, comfortable home. That it became. Jackie gave it such warmth that people were often visibly moved at the feeling inside the house. I eventually came to be reasonably satisfied with it. But after three years there, I still found myself occasionally noticing how it just wasn't imposing at all.

You see what a constant unrelenting fight it is for the coronary personality to make changes? The good side, though, is that while I was in many ways still the same person I was able to make some major decisions in more sensible directions. It was a lot easier on my arteries occasionally to worry that I wasn't impressing people enough instead of each month having to find the money for a house payment twice what I could afford.

I was still having trouble finding the kind of friends I wanted in the university community. In the English Department, no one shared my interests in hunting and fishing. So I sought out some of the people in the Commerce Department and made friends with Dean Palmer, Hal Holen, Harvey Larson, Tom Wells, Chuck Lein, Al Day, Charlie Hash, and Mrs. Robinson. They were my coffee companions. But they had their friendships pretty well set, so there was some limit on how far I could go.

On the Bozeman *Chronicle* there was an outdoor columnist, Rolf Olson. He shot a 7-mm. Magnum big-game rifle, as I did. I loaded my own ammunition and had a special long-range sight for my gun. I called Rolf on the phone one day and introduced myself. I suggested we go shooting together. We met and went to the long-distance rifle range in Logan.

We found we had many common interests in the outdoors and started visiting back and forth. We hunted together and spent many evenings talking. Because I couldn't walk in the mountains, we decided to buy horses and soon Rolf and I had horses and a trailer.

He taught me many things and was a good friend. I had said at the Emotions Anonymous meeting that I was ready for a closer emotional relationship. With Rolf and Kenny I was as close as I was able to be at the time. I encouraged Rolf to apply at the university to teach writing. He joined the staff, so I had a good friend in the department. Rolf decided to marry a mutual friend and asked me to be his best man, which was an honor because I had never been close enough to anyone to be asked before.

Slowly and tentatively I was starting to try to build a community for myself and my family. Like any first steps they were faltering and weak. I was painfully aware how slowly and weakly things were going, but I had to stay with it and face the fact I was doing the best I could. Again, all I had to sustain me was the question, "Is this what I believe in most for me?" And it was.

I knew I was working on building a community here. But I didn't realize how hard I was working on other things, too. Within the next year, my second in Montana, I would be embarked on two new careers. The strange thing was, I had absolutely no idea those deep, fundamental interests were even in me. They were deep and so much a part of me, yet they were so close in that I took them for granted.

The telling of the story goes fast but that second year was the result of the previous six years of trying to find what I believed in by following my nose. You might look carefully at what happened to me to see if it could give you a better idea of trying to find what you believe in and trusting in where that takes you.

During my first year at Montana State, I was working on the problem of finding better ways to teach writing. I had met Earl Ringo, Dean of the College of Education. He was interested in my ideas on writing and on the psychology of teaching. He had asked me to take part of his class time in summer session to speak to his graduate students on how to face our fear of ourselves in teaching.

I had a fine time talking to his students, I made a number of friends but two were especially crucial: one was Gerry Sullivan, the other was Merlin Willett. Over the years Gerry has become one of the closest friends I've ever had. Merlin Willett was a nursing graduate student and had me speak to the Nurses' District Association on my feelings about death as I went through my heart attack and surgery. I also spoke of my great appreciation and love for the nurses who had taken such good care of me. Out of this speech came a chance about six months later to speak at Whitefish, Montana, to nurses from a four-state area.

The second year at Montana State University I continued to teach writing, which I enjoyed doing, especially freshman writing. But Earl Ringo asked me to teach a class in educational psychology winter and spring quarter. I was happy to have this chance to discuss the ways I had applied my psychology education and life experiences to teaching.

The first two times I taught prospective teachers their first course I didn't have much of an idea of what I really believed. But I had enough courage by then and I had Earl's support so that I tried to find my own way. Also, Gordon Simpson was teaching the course. He had a background in counseling that was very different from mine, but he had much the same approach.

I also had a piece of good fortune. I was curious about the value of the typical material included in most psychology courses for teachers. So I made up two final examinations with questions drawn at random from the test questions furnished by Cronbach, the author of the text I was using. I gave one final exam on the first day of class. Then I taught the students the material as well as I could and gave the second final exam. I was able to get only a very modest increase in the scores. This happened because so much of what the students showed in their finals they had when they started the class. Also, much of the conventional material was of such questionable value that it was hard to motivate the students to high levels of achievement.

This was a crucial experience for me because it demonstrated how little teaching of factual material goes on during a quarter. Yet, we usually don't recognize this fact. By giving a final exam the first day, I was able to see the small gain. This helped me see that most anything else I wanted to do would be at least as useful if not much more so.

Someone brought to my attention a book on teaching by Arthur Coombs, *The Professional Education of a Teacher.* Coombs pointed out research that indicated that both the good and the poor teacher knew what they should do. The only problem was that the poor teacher couldn't do it. So his emphasis was on giving students as much experience in the human relations aspects of teaching as possible so they could do a better job. His basic point to teachers, nurses and parents is that "the self is the instrument." That was the same idea I had been working on without those words.

My students also guided me with the cards they wrote. Each day at the beginning of class there would be a pile of cards and notes on my table at the front of the room waiting to be read and commented on. I respected those statements, feelings, and questions from my students as if

they were Holy Writ. Because of the respect I showed
their cards, my students spent a great deal of time and
care thinking about the course and helped me fashion it
out of chaos. Some of my students had been in my freshman writing classes, so they were especially helpful because they already knew me. It was an exciting time.

In May, as I was in the middle of my second time
teaching educational psychology, I was asked to speak to
a continuing education program for nurses from a four-
state area at Big Mountain, near Whitefish, Montana.

Here again, I was lucky. I was to speak over a two-
and-one-half-day period. I had my wife with me. And I
had the support of some nurses who really believed in me,
like Rita Darragh. From only God knows where, I got the
courage to avoid an academic approach to my subject and
took a human one.

I had been asked to speak to the nurses on communication. I'm sure many of them expected me to draw
on my experiences as an advertising man, a speech teacher, and a writing teacher. While I had no idea how deep it
went at the time, I had more important ideas in me about
communication that were just waiting to get out.

Because those ideas had been forming over so long a
time and were now ready to come out, they would not be
denied.

I found myself saying to the nurses that 90 per cent of
successful communication comes from having a good
heart toward the other person. Only the last 10 per cent
has to do with techniques like using simple words and
short sentences. Also, with people who have good hearts
toward each other, if there is some technical communication problem, their goodheartedness toward each
other will make it easy to identify and clear up the
problem.

How can we develop this good heart toward others?
Simply by getting a good heart toward ourselves. I found
myself telling the nurses of deep thinking I had been

doing that I was only dimly aware of. I spoke of my difficulties of accepting myself, accepting others, facing any anger and fear and not pushing those feelings off on others. I spoke of how my expectations of another person had so much to do with what I later found in that other person. I spoke of the problems I had accepting my sexual nature and I told of my basic ideas on changing the things I could change in myself and selecting the environments most conducive to my growth and well-being.

And all the time, those fifty great faces with their warmth, acceptance, and love were communicating to me, "Jess, you have touched our hearts, continue on as you see fit."

In the evenings Jackie and I discussed what to do as we walked the ski hill in the warm mountain air. It was one of those magical times that are usually so short but in this case lasted two and one half days. There were some nun nurses in the group, but when the time came to speak of sex, I was able to do it without being intimidated or frightened into posturing because of the habits those nuns wore.

I told those women how too much fear of their sexuality could cause them so much trouble in their supervisory roles. I told them of Zorba the Greek's compassion for women and of the Jewish Talmud's insistence that sex is something women have a right to and that the husband must oblige. I told them it was as if when a woman married she was to be given a whistle by her husband and that whistle had absolute control of their sex life. When she blew that whistle, her husband was to come a-running.

The last morning I wound up my talks and was very moved by the opportunity to be with those great women. I went around the circle and shook each one's hand and came back to the front of the room. I turned around to find them on their feet applauding. Some of them had gone to town the night before and gotten whistles, which they were blowing. One little nun was blowing her whistle so hard her cheeks were red. It was a strange situation for a Norwegian farm boy to find himself in.

The nurses took opportunities to tell me they had all felt the same way I did, but so few people had said those things to them before. From the way they responded, Jackie and I realized I had said a book. Thank God for Mary Burke, who had taken the whole meeting down on her tape recorder so I could write my first book off her tapes.

The point of my story is that it wasn't until I had worked a long time on following my nose and asking, "Hey, God, what should I do now?" that these things could happen.

I had been working out my book in my head for years and yet I wasn't even aware it was there. Jackie and I had talked about the ideas countless times, so I wasn't saying anything we hadn't talked about over and over again. Thus to say I wrote the book off tapes could give a wrong impression. I can't dictate a letter without wandering, to say nothing of a book. But this was different. Without knowing it, I had carefully thought out everything I had said.

Actually writing that book down from the tapes as I had said it was hard for me because I felt the ghosts of English professors past and present looking over my shoulder. I was ashamed of the simplicity and roughness I saw in my writing. But I wanted to write that book so the people who read it would get the feeling of me speaking to them as it was when I talked to the nurses. Usually I was able to handle my fear and keep the spontaneity of my talks.

It wasn't until I heard myself talking in the tapes and wrote it down that I realized what I really believed. It was such a strange feeling to find so much that was so close to me that I hadn't even been very aware of or appreciated.

Just a few months earlier I had been anxious about

being promoted so I made a list of nineteen articles I could write on research I had done and other interests I had. The amazing thing to me is that none of the ideas in my first book were on that list of nineteen articles. In searching for my "acres of diamonds" I was looking in the wrong place—and ignoring my own back yard. That lesson more than any other has taught me the tremendous value of letting go and not trying to overplan or force things too much.

I went right from the experience of writing my book to my summer session educational psychology class. It was the most exciting I have ever taught. I came to class each day so full of things to say. My ideas were fresh in me and I was bursting with them.

One day I was telling my students that I didn't like the title I had planned to use for my book, *Grow or Die*. I thought it was too hard. They agreed. I asked what the title should be. They said *I Ain't Much, Baby—But I'm All I Got*. This was a phrase a friend, Bill Gove, had given me. I said it was too long. They said it didn't matter, use it. So I did.

One of my students was Jack Jefferies, a forty-five-year-old ex-Skaggs Drug manager who quit and came back to school to be a teacher. Jack said in a paper about that class: "Coming to class and seeing us all work together is so beautiful. It's breath-taking just as seeing the Spanish Peaks at sunrise is breath-taking." It was that kind of experience for me, too. I still see many of the people from that class regularly. We are a part of each other's lives. I look back on that time as being more like a religious experience for me than a class.

By this time I had my book typed up and sent off to a publisher. I was also teaching a small adult class of fourteen teachers. They wanted copies of my book and didn't want to wait until it was published. I told them I could get them a xerox copy for $5 and passed a sheet around for their orders. All fourteen wanted a copy. I then found the $5 per copy estimate that was given me too low, so I used their money to help pay for running off two hundred mimeograph copies, because I thought some of my other students and the nurses might want copies. So I put the extras in the bookstore and they sold out in a short time. I ran two hundred more, then four hundred at a time. Then I went to a commercial printer because it was too much trouble to mimeograph. Some of the other bookstores started selling the book and we started getting mail orders from all over the United States just through word of mouth.

I sold many thousands of copies of that book out of my home. The letters I got from all across the United States, foreign countries, jails, and mental institutions confirmed what the nurses had told me. My readers got the message I wanted to communicate.

That first rough manuscript started me writing. My educational psychology class started a deeper search for answers to crucial questions. I was able to see that psychology is people, and as Skinner says, if it doesn't work for one pigeon, it won't work for the average of one thousand pigeons. So I walk into my classroom each day ready to find what might be there and trying to really see with fresh eyes.

But this great, magical way of surrendering to life isn't easy. It is terribly hard. No sooner had I got the knack of it than I lost it again. I now think we will always keep losing this knack, but each time we try we can get it back more easily and keep it longer.

By the time I came back to school in the fall something was wrong with my head. I think what happened was I let my ego carry me away again and I started believing I was God. I was going to solve all the problems of the world. The Big I. The result was a lot of sick games. I came at people as if I had the secret of their deliverance. They had better pay close attention because I was only going to give them one chance. Although a few very fine things happened that quarter, there was lots of crap and I screwed up royally.

Winter quarter I was planning to say the revised version of my book to my students. I knew how important the opportunity was, so I fought to keep those eighteen hours of lectures free of the sickness that was creeping up on me. Many people who have read the published version of my previous book say I did pretty well. It's a wonder because I was in trouble.

I started spring quarter feeling poorly and got worse. I went horseback riding to see if that would help. It did momentarily, but that was all. My wife wanted me to see the doctor. One night my oldest daughter, Janet, said, "Dad, you don't look well, you should see the doctor." The next morning I went. X rays showed there was a big growth in my stomach that could be a ballooned artery or a tumor. I had to fly to Minneapolis to the hospital that evening. I went home, found Jackie, and got ready to leave. Things didn't look good, but it turned out they would soon look a lot worse.

12

Jackie

In late April of 1970, the whole family realized Dad was sick again. Everything about Jess was haywire; his personality was different, physically he was different, mentally he was different. I begged him to see a doctor on the last Sunday in April. He was crabby with me and I stormed back upstairs and flopped on the bed crying—just like in the movies.

Downstairs I heard Janet talking to her father. "Dad, there's something wrong with you, you've got to go to the doctor." Jess couldn't say no to his eldest daughter.

The night before Jess and I had been to a party. Jess couldn't eat any hors d'oeuvres. This was weird. Jess usually ate more snacks than most people eat for dinner. An hour later we had come home from the party because Jess was ill. This too was unheard of. Because of these things we were putting the pressure on him to see a doctor.

On Sunday afternoon Jess went out in the country to ride his horse, Whiskey. Whiskey was the joy of Jess's

life. Jess found the horse at the local sale barn. He was a
bedraggled-looking mess. Jess bought him for $150. He
was a hot horse, probably for sale because he was too
much horse instead of too little. Once he was fed well and
groomed, one could see that this horse was mostly thoroughbred.

Once on Whiskey, Jess was gone. Whiskey would run
up a mountainside and still be ready for more when he
was at the top.

Late in the afternoon Jess came home with color in his
face and feeling better. I still insisted he see a doctor on
Monday.

Monday morning came and Jess drove to the doctor's
office. I stayed home relatively unconcerned.

Just before noon, Jess came in the door. One look at
his face and I knew all was not well.

"I have to fly to Minneapolis today. There's something
in my stomach. The doctor thinks it might be an aneurysm." Jess began to cry.

I began to cry, too. "Not again, God, not again." I
went to the phone and called the doctor.

"Jess has something in there that showed on X ray. It
might be an aneurysm on the aorta. This is a ballooning
out of the wall of the aorta. It is very dangerous. I want
him to go back to the heart surgeons right away. I've already talked to them, they are expecting him."

I called the airport. Jess could get on the 8 P.M. flight
to Minneapolis.

The day was cold and blustering. We had been having
a late spring blizzard. The weather matched our feelings
perfectly.

I went next door to Dave and Mel Sullivan's. In the
past few years we had become as close as two couples can
get. We shared our joys and sorrows, our triumphs and
tragedies; the mixed blessings of raising teen-agers. We
love that couple as though they were family.

I told Mel what had happened. She comforted me. Dave agreed to drive us to the airport. I was not taking the same flight as Jess, I planned on waiting to see what the doctors would decide. I needed time to settle the children. Nevertheless, Dave didn't want me to drive alone.

At seven o'clock we left for the airport. The children kissed their father goodbye. They didn't know how serious Jess's problem might be.

The night was a bad one. Northwest Orient's 727 arrived. Snow arrived with it. Just as Jess was going up the steps of the aircraft, the flight was canceled. We decided to drive to Billings. There were more flights from Billings, and there the weather was better.

To get out of Bozeman going east one must go over the Bozeman Pass. There is a freeway there, but the pass is still a bad one and right on the pass there is only a two-lane road. We drove eastward. The pass was clear. In fact, the whole 150 miles were clear. We were just ahead of the storm.

We got to Billings and found that there was an early morning flight to Minneapolis. We got Jess booked on the flight. We drove to Aunt Margaret Wick's house. Aunt Margaret and Uncle Lloyd were gracious. They had a bed for Jess.

Dave and I had a cup of coffee and with misgivings we left Jess and started the long ride back to Bozeman. It was almost eleven o'clock by then. With luck we would be back in Bozeman by 2 A.M.

Dave was an excellent driver. It was so nice to be able to relax in the car and not worry.

Soon after leaving Billings, the snow hit. We were driving into the teeth of a howling Montana blizzard. We drove slowly into a white blanket. We could hardly see the edge of the road. At two o'clock we were still fifty miles from home. We still had the Bozeman Pass ahead of us. Dave and I talked, we fiddled with the radio. I picked up WCCO, a Minneapolis radio station. There was the familiar voice of Franklin Hobbs, the all-night disc jockey. The weather was clear and warm in Minneapolis.

We hit the pass. We drove as fast as Dave dared. Halfway up the pass we could not go forward any more. We slid backward down the pass looking for a place to turn around. There was none. We backed some more. At the bottom of the pass, Dave got out in the snow to get the chains from the trunk. For some reason, I cannot now remember, I had no trunk key. Dave was a gentleman. Although he had smoke coming out of his ears, he only smiled. We decided to make one more run at the pass. We slipped sideways, we whirled back, but we kept making progress. By sheer will power we got to the top of the pass and were almost home.

We drove into our driveway at 4 A.M. Dave went home for some much needed sleep. He had to be work by 7:30 A.M. I went into my house and climbed into a warm tub. I was cold and tired and very worried. I knew there was no sense in going to bed. I was too tense to sleep.

In the morning I got all of the children off to school.

Shortly after nine o'clock, Mel arrived with her coffee cup. We talked. Or rather, I talked. Mel listened. I called Billings. Jess did not make the 6 A.M. flight. It, too, was canceled. He was leaving about one that afternoon.

I called the heart specialist in Minneapolis. Jess's doctor was not in; I talked to his new partner, a man I had never met. "If Jess has an aneurysm, we will probably operate immediately."

I called the airport for reservations on the 8 P.M. flight. The weather was clearing. I had to find someone to help with the children.

Mel was working—she had just taken the day off to be with me—so I couldn't ask her. I called around. There were no baby-sitters available. I called a friend of Jess's. Rolf and Rainie agreed to come over and help. My good friend Lorraine McEwen, Rainie's mother, said she would help if she could. I packed my suitcase.

The eight o'clock flight left on time. The snow had stopped. The weather ahead looked good. My brother John met me at the airport. It was good to see a familiar face. The temperature in Minneapolis was in the eighties.

I learned that Jess was safe in St. Mary's Hospital. I went home to John's, where his dear little wife Janet had a bed ready for me. I slept soundly, for I had not been to bed for forty-two hours.

In the week to come Jess had tests and tests. The doctors were vague. They planned to operate, but they kept testing. I could not pin any doctor down. Thinking back, I remember that I did not try very hard. I had a vague presentiment that I did not want to know very much.

I had one clue about what was growing in Jess's body. His chart was left open one day at the nurse's station. Clipped there in his chart were two photographs. There was an enormous foreign-looking growth showing just below his ribs. I know nothing about X rays, but I knew that that "thing," larger than an orange but smaller than a breadbox, was not natural. I stared and then walked away. I must put the forbidden peek out of my mind.

Tuesday arrived. Jess was to go to surgery at noon.

When Jess had his heart surgery, for some unknown reason, he was not given his hypo before he was taken down to the operating room. Once there, he lay in the hallway for quite some time, wide awake. We insisted that this not happen again.

Jess's hypo arrived, he again climbed on a cart. This time I rode the elevator with him and went right into the pre-operating room with him. We hadn't long to wait. I kissed him goodbye and returned to that familiar surgery waiting room on the third floor. It was twelve-fifteen.

Jess's mother was there, my brother John was there. About three, John left to go to the office to do some work. John was a brand-new attorney; he had just passed his bar exam the previous week. My mother came. It was four o'clock, still no word. I looked through the waiting room door and saw one of Jess's nurses from the past week walk into the intensive care suite. Soon she came out, her right hand shielding her face; she was crying. I took this clue into my internal computer and stored it beside my memory of the pictures in Jess's medical record. I said nothing. I waited. Five o'clock, six o'clock. Jess's brother, Jim, arrived.

At seven o'clock I went into the intensive care rooms looking for someone who would tell me something. I found Dr. Mazzitello. "What is wrong with Jess? No one has told me anything." He looked up. "Come on, Jackie, we'll go find Dr. Garamella.'" We walked back through the intensive care doors. Miraculously there stood Dr. Garamella. He was looking for me.

"Come on in this room, Jackie. I want to talk to you."

I didn't want to go. I knew the news was bad. After heart surgery he told me good news in the hall. Now he wanted to take me behind the nurse's station to the nurses' conference room. My knees felt like jelly, my throat began to have that familiar dry feeling.

Just then my brother John stepped off the elevator. I grabbed his hand and pulled him after me. We stepped into that private room.

"Sit down, Jackie," said Dr. Garamella as he pulled out a chair at the conference table. I sat down. He sat on my left at the head of the table. John sat down on my right.

Dr. Garamella held out his hand. I took it. "Jess has a growth in there. It is very large. It is attached to all the major organs on the right side of his body." Dr. Garamella's face was pained. I squeezed his hand harder.

"Did you get the growth out?" John was speaking almost in a whisper.

"We couldn't remove it. We had to leave it."

I twisted the doctor's fingers. He didn't move. I knew

what the next question was. I knew I had to ask it, I didn't want to. Finally, "Is it cancer?"

"Yes, Jackie, that is what took so long. The pathologists have been studying the tissue." Dr. Garamella looked terrible.

I remember kneading his hands. I was pulling and twisting them. "God, your wonderful surgeon's hands, look what I'm doing to them." There I was being theatrical. I still blush about that statement.

I asked the next obvious question. "How long?"

"We think not long. The pathologists think it is a very fast-growing malignancy."

John was strangling beside me. "Does Jess know?"

"Yes, he asked to be told right away. We told him while he was still pretty groggy. I don't know if he will remember or not."

Dr. Garamella sat exhausted. I twisted his fingers some more. They were a life line. I did not want to let go. How could we bear this? After saving Jess's life with heart surgery, here we were, just three years later, facing a certain death with cancer. Inoperable cancer. I was numb with grief and shock.

My thoughts began to come. They were sensible, steady thoughts. I did not have the feeling of hysteria that I had had eight years before when Jess had his early heart attack. I took a deep breath and freed the imprisoned doctor. He could not help me any more. I must get about the business of telling Jess's mother and brother. My mother, too.

Dr. Garamella left, a sadder man. I am sure he too felt the irony of pulling Jess through heart surgery only to lose him to cancer.

I asked John to go tell the family in the waiting room and bring them here. Jess's mother walked in looking gray and numb. She sat down quietly. My mother arrived, tears in her eyes. Jim came. He looked especially bad. His wife, Ann, had had surgery for cancer of the colon this past year. Ann's mother was dying of cancer even then. We were all tense and strained.

My thoughts were with our children in Montana. I did not want them to hear this news from a stranger. I decided that someone from the family must fly out and tell them. A few tears came. My mother in her fright was trying to comfort me. I could not stand this intrusion into my privacy.

"Mother, will you for God's sake sit down and leave me alone." I was instantly sorry. My mother, with her unique ability to feel sorrow for everyone, was just asking me to comfort Jess's mother. She was so alone. I reached over and gave Jess's mother, Bertha, a hug. She, too, was beyond comfort. Bertha and I were surrounded by family, but we were having to face this problem each one alone. There is no comfort for this finality.

The inevitable nurse arrived. There was another room we were moved to. It was the room that the grieving parents of the baby who had died in heart surgery three years before had occupied. I hated that room instantly but we all went into it. It was a long, narrow room with a studio couch and some chairs. It was cheerless.

I had no desire to see Jess. I could not cope with that yet. I sat numb and alone. Here and there I heard a sniffle and a small groan. Everyone was grieving. I could not cry, I had too much to figure out.

Another nurse arrived. "Your husband is awake and asking for you." I had to go. With dragging steps I walked into the intensive care unit. I saw Ginny, the nurse who had been on duty when Jess had his heart surgery. I gave no sign that I saw her. I just walked zombie-like behind the white-clad legs to Jess's room. Once again he was in a four-bed ward. I had no interest in the other patients. I walked through the large room to Jess's bed on the right by the window. I leaned over and kissed Jess.

I had a vague feeling of revulsion. This was my husband again, but he was a stranger yet another time.

Cancer. There is something weird and foreign about cancer to me. I found I could not accept cancer as easily as I could accept heart. With heart there always seemed to be hope. Here there seemed to be none.

"Did the doctors tell you what was wrong?" Jess was asking this question with a frightened, pleading look on his face.

"Yes, Jess, they did."

"What did they say?" I could not tell him. I would not tell him. If what the doctors told him in the recovery room didn't register, I wasn't about to say it.

I ran out into the hall. "Ginny, Jess is asking what's wrong with him, I don't want to tell him, come and talk to him."

Ginny walked back into the room with me. She did a very wonderful thing. Ginny climbed right up into the bed with Jess and took him into her arms. "Come on, now, Jess, I watched you beat a lot tougher thing than this, you're going to be all right."

Jess wept. I wept. Ginny, too, had tears in her eyes. Jess knew. I didn't need to tell him. He dozed off.

I went back to the waiting room. A woman who was unknown to me was asking at the desk for word of Jess. I had told the staff that no one was to know or be told even the least little thing about Jess. The nurses were being properly evasive.

I walked up to this stranger. "I am Mrs. Lair; what is it you want?"

She was a member of the nursing faculty from Bozeman. She was here studying at the University of Minnesota. "The faculty at Bozeman asked me to find out how Dr. Lair is."

Calmly I lied. "Dr. Lair is fine. There was no problem.

He will be going home soon." Satisfied or not, the woman left.

I was determined that no one would know before the children. I could not stand for a thoughtless phone call of sympathy. In a small town these things happen easily.

A nurse arrived with pillows and blankets. "You should sleep, Mrs. Lair."

"I will go to my brother's home to sleep." The nurse gasped. Everyone expected me to stay near Jess.

In the awful finality of my discussion with Dr. Garamella I was already a widow. I had to protect myself for the children. I would leave this hellish place for the peace of my brother's house. Jess was sedated. I could not play the game of grieving at his side. I must get away and think and restore myself.

My brother drove me home. My mother had gone there previously. I began to lay plans. John would fly to Bozeman to tell the children. He is a tender, sensitive man. I feel that he is most like me of all my family. He would do that evil job as kindly as possible.

I greeted my grieving family in an oddly peaceful way. I was absent-minded of their presence. I was living totally inside my own soul. I found strength there that had come since the heart surgery days. I would survive there for many days to come.

I did not ask John to go to Bozeman, I told him that he must do this for me. He agreed. He would leave on Thursday afternoon. This was Tuesday evening. I had to get through Wednesday and Thursday without letting anyone know of our new sorrow.

The children did not know that anything was wrong. I later learned that Jess, Jr., was suspicious for a reason beyond my control. When surgery dragged on that afternoon, I, for reasons I do not understand, decided to phone the children and tell them everything was all right. I dialed our number in Montana off and on for two hours. I asked the operator for help. I found that there are only two trunk lines into Montana. Both were jammed for some reason. I sent a telegram telling them surgery was over and nothing was wrong. Had I been able to telephone I might have been believed more readily. A telegram aroused our eldest son's suspicions.

I went to bed that Tuesday night and slept. I slept soundly. A blessing from God.

Wednesday I went to the hospital. Jess's mother and Jim's wife, Ann, were there. Ann was distraught, her own cancer surgery fresh in her mind. I could not comfort her.

I went in to Jess. I kissed him and held his hand. He was restless and frightened. I could not help him. He desperately wanted life. Only God could grant him that. My heart was torn in two. My serenity began to slip and I fled.

Out in the waiting room I went right into the bathroom and washed my hands. I returned and sat for a few minutes. Again, I went to the bathroom and washed my hands. I stopped.

There in the bathroom I had to come to terms with cancer. It was a God-damned dirty disease to me. I felt as though my husband was unclean. Heart was an organ that sometimes wore out. Cancer was a dirty, filthy foreign invader of my husband's beloved body. I felt as though cancer was communicable. I did not want cancer, therefore I did not want to touch my husband with any intimacy. A pat on the shoulder, a kiss on the cheek was all I wanted to give him, and that as seldom as possible.

Others have told me of seeing or feeling reactions close to mine.

I heard of one man who ceased to visit his wife of twenty-five years while she was in the hospital with cancer.

I know a young mother who was horrified to find that many of her friends would not let their children come over to see her young son, who had leukemia.

Another woman whose husband was in the hospital

with cancer at the same time Jess was walked into her husband's room with a handkerchief over her mouth and nose.

I don't know if these are extreme examples or not, but I do feel that there is a "communicable air" about cancer that one understands only by going through it.

I knew this would not do. I came to terms with myself that Wednesday morning in the bathroom. I walked out the bathroom door into the intensive care suite and down to Jess's room. I took him in my arms and held him. My fear would not die, but I owed it to this beautiful man to conquer that fear and to give him the love and closeness that he needed.

I stayed at the hospital all day. A television set in the waiting room told of the tragedies at Kent State. I was too removed to empathize. I received a call from Bozeman. I lied quite effectively, but it was difficult.

I returned to my brother's home. My mother joined me in the other bed in the downstairs guest room. I was just dozing off, my defenses were lowered. "My God, Mother, I am going to be a widow." My mother went to pieces. It is a special sadness, I think, for a mother to see her child become a widow before her time. I tried to comfort Mom. We slept.

Thursday afternoon John caught the plane for Montana. Later that day Jess was moved from intensive care to an upper floor of the hospital. Most hospital floors at St. Mary's hospital are reasonably happy places. This floor was not. The chemistry of the nursing staff was such that this floor was a miserable one to be on. I believe it must have been a miserable place to work, also. All the staff was tense and irritable. I determined to get Jess on a happy floor. I would not have this poor atmosphere added to our burdens.

In an article in *McCall's* Magazine for October 1966 entitled "The Turning Points of Life," by Gerald Caplan, M.D., and Vivian Codden, I read about passive reaction versus reacting with action. The conclusions drawn were that a person in crisis who reacts with action, one who badgers the doctors, talks about her problem with openness, who weeps and expresses her fright, passes through the crisis with fewer problems in the future than the passive reactor.

I have been a passive reactor through many crises. I was most passive and amenable to the doctors and the hospital staff when our handicapped daughter was born. I then needed psychiatric help.

I reacted inwardly when Jess had his heart attack and we moved to the farm, and I ended up in a psychiatric hospital.

With the cancer scare I openly expressed my fears. I would not be stifled by the hospital rules. I made known how I felt a little better to the people around me. And I was rewarded by feeling better, and taking this shattering event with relative equanimity.

It is not an easy task to learn to let one's hair down and to express one's fears more openly. But I now am positive that this is the only course of action.

Of course, in the traumas of my younger life, I was so shut off from my true feelings that I *could* not express them; it was not that I *would* not express them.

I also think it is time that most of us start taking a more active role in managing our health care.

Too many of us are like sheep when we are confronted by doctors. To my thinking, this puts a burden on the doctors that they do not really want either.

Any doctor worthy of his degree is willing to work *with* us rather than *for* us when illness strikes.

There are many decisions that are really up to *us* to make. In order to do this intelligently, we must have as many of the facts about our loved one's illness as possible. If a doctor would not supply answers to my questions, I would seek another doctor.

In our case, we have been fortunate to have patient,

kind doctors who were willing to answer all queries; thus we were partakers in our medical care rather than by-standers.

The twelve steps of Emotions Anonymous have given me a tool to use to be open to my feelings. The twelve steps, when I practice them, keep me in tune with myself and help me to deal with my feelings on a day-to-day basis. I therefore am not always bogged down with stifled emotions that have no outlet.

Soon the doctors arrived, with news. Further study of the tissue by the pathologists had caused a change in the diagnosis. The doctors now felt that instead of a fast-growing malignancy, Jess had a Hodgkin's-type tumor and with cobalt and such he could live for a few years instead of the weeks we were planning on.

I rejoiced and went to the phone. I had to reach John so that he could revise his thinking when he told the children.

I had Jess moved down to the third-floor post-operative wing. This was where he had successfully recovered from heart surgery. I began to tell people what had happened. I phoned many old friends and shared our sorrow. Everyone was supportive. I continued on, wrapped in grief.

As the days went by Jess became more and more agitated and depressed. I could not comfort him. Here we were so desperately in need of one another, but our shock and revulsion were tearing us apart. This was different from the heart surgery.

Sunday morning arrived. My father had driven down from Duluth to take my mother back home. My father is a silent, handsome man. He never has much to say. We said little to each other. He communicated his deep sorrow without the need of words. I knew how he felt. There had been much between my parents and me. We had come to an understanding these past few years. We were silent together.

I said a choked goodbye to my parents and left for the hospital. The doctors entered Jess's room shortly after I arrived.

Jess's agitation was extreme. "I don't know what tranquilizers you're giving me, but double the dose." Jess had even contemplated diving out a window to escape the horror of cancer. I understood.

The doctor wrote in Jess's medical record. The intern who was with Dr. Garamella looked over his shoulder and pointed at a page. Dr. Garamella read. He looked up amazed.

"The pathologists have had a meeting and now feel the tissue is benign." The doctors were happy to deliver that sentence, yet it took some bravery, considering our suffering these past days.

I assumed the doctors were lying to relieve Jess's anxiety. I felt sure Jess would not be fooled.

I stepped out into the hall behind them. "What gives?"

Dr. Garamella said that what he had told Jess and me was true. The pathologists had had a tissue conference. Two pathologists from the university had felt that Jess's tumor was caused by a rare overwhelming virus of the lymphatic system. This disease had often been mistaken for cancer in the past. The St. Mary's pathologists then concurred. A sample of the tissue from Jess's tumor was being sent to Marquette University and to the Armed Forces Tissue Institute at Bethesda. The doctors would abide by their decision.

I thought about this startling news. I decided to go along with the doctors in their belief that an error had been made. Deep inside I decided to wait until I had heard from Bethesda. I had been through too much. I couldn't jump from one belief to another quite as readily as I pretended. I had paid too dear a price. I could not raise my hopes once again if Bethesda decided it was cancer after all. The doctors were sure now the tumor was benign. But they had been just as sure it was malignant. Inside I waited.

The external side of me rushed to a phone and called the news to my brother. I called Bozeman and told the children. The doctors said I could take Jess home when he was stronger. We would be coming sometime the next week.

Once Jess heard and accepted that he did not have cancer, he began to function once again. He was eager to be near the mountains he had thought he would never see again. We began to prepare for the flight home.

By Wednesday, just eight days after hearing that he was a dead man, Jess had talked the doctors into releasing him. I took him to my brother's home. We would leave Minneapolis on the afternoon flight on Thursday.

The previous night I had bought Jess a Neil Diamond record. Jess liked this young lad's music. He found many messages in the words that Neil Diamond wrote and sang so well.

At John and Janet's house, Jess and I were once again as before. I don't know even know what possessed us. I put "Holly Holy" on the stereo. Jess and I stood in the middle of the floor hanging on to each other and swaying to the music. We were dancing a slow, weak dance filled with the sorrow, fear, horror, and now joy of the past and present. I heard a strangled sob. Janet Carey had peeked through the kitchen door and seen us. It was more than she could bear.

I put Jess to bed in John and Janet's bedroom. He was not there for more than a few minutes when the nausea that had tortured him for weeks overcame him.

We both knew he still belonged in the hospital but we were determined to get back to Montana and the children.

I phoned the doctor. I had worked as a medical technician twenty years before. I knew how to give hypos. The doctor ordered a medicine to combat the nausea. I gave Jess the first of many shots and he was able to rest.

As we boarded our flight Thursday afternoon I was frightened. Jess looked like a concentration camp expatriate. He was all eyes and bones. He looked very, very old.

We flew to Billings. At Billings Jess quietly asked me to get him some crackers. He thought crackers might stop the nausea that was beginning to overwhelm him. We were afraid we would be bumped off the plane. He had to hang on until Bozeman, just thirty minutes away.

Aloft and flying high over the beginning of the Rockies, Jess could take no more. He collapsed. The stewardesses moved us forward into first class. They removed the armrests and pushed the seats down. Jess was given oxygen. I gave him another hypo. Nothing worked.

The pilot radioed ahead for our doctor in Bozeman. We flew on. Everyone was frightened, especially Jess, Jr., on the ground in Bozeman. In our small airport one can hear everything. He heard there was a sick man aboard. He heard the airlines call our doctor. He knew his dad was sick on that airplane.

The minutes dragged. We landed at last in Bozeman and an ambulance drove out to the plane. We were home, but Jess hardly knew. Jess, Jr., strode manfully aboard. He was very tall and trying to look and act like an adult. He succeeded with his usual grace.

Jess was carried out of the plane in a funny webbed seat used for such emergencies. The ambulance drove off. I hugged one of the stewardesses who had been especially kind. Jess, Jr., and I walked to our car.

At the hospital Jess was feeling better. He was too weak to have made that thousand-mile trip, but we had fooled the doctors and we were back in Bozeman.

It was the middle of May. Only two shorts weeks since our departure, yet we were never to be the same again.

Summer had arrived in our absence. We flew out in blizzards and returned to 70° days.

Of the weeks and months ahead I shall say little. We had good days and bad.

I wanted to believe Jess was well, and yet other symptoms beset him. His right leg swelled horribly. I had heard this was a further symptom of Hodgkin's, when the lymph glands swell.

Our Bozeman doctor recommended a return to Minneapolis in the middle of June when the swelling didn't subside. We perversely drove instead to the Oregon coast. We had never seen the Pacific Ocean together. We thoroughly enjoyed our days on the sandy beach.

After three days of ocean we drove home. Jess's leg was worse. We rested for two days and, taking the children with us this time, we drove to Minneapolis.

While at home we heard from Marquette University that Jess's tumor was benign. Bethesda was still silent, though it had been a month. I was still worried.

We arrived in Minneapolis. Jess's leg was swollen because he had a blood clot that went from the top of his knee to his groin. It could have killed him driving to Oregon and back!

Jess again went into the hospital for several weeks, and during this time we heard from Bethesda. The tumor was benign! I could believe for sure now.

The doctors poked at his stomach to feel the size of the tumor. The tumor was not there.

How to explain it? To quote a nursing sister of the Order of St. Joseph, which ran St. Mary's Hospital, "You must believe in miracles, there is no explanation known to man. We all prayed Dr. Lair well." Again, I believed.

Jess was returned from the dead!

13

Jess

Looking back, I think I might have been able to come to an acceptance of my death in the three weeks of life it seemed I had. But I would have had to come to that acceptance at my own pace. And I might not have made it. Even if I hadn't come to that acceptance, I still think I might have died fairly peacefully because so often I've seen that death brings its own numbing and sense of peace.

But that's all speculation and I'm glad I didn't have to find out. An old priest said once that we don't die until our soul is at its best from God's point of view. I guess God saw my soul needed a lot more work.

It seemed as if that sickness broke a different kind of sick chain for me. By the time the summer was over I was ready to go back to school and teach in a better way. I found that when I went in the classroom that fall I seemed to be free of some of what must have been very sick needs, because I found my students responded much better to my teaching.

It is hard for me to describe the past two and one half years since my cancer scare. They have been as formless as I could make them and so much has happened. If there is one word for what I have been working on in those years, it is the word "surrender." As often as I can, five minutes at a time, I've been saying, "Hey, God, what should I do now? How should I respond to this situation I'm in?" It has helped.

It hasn't been easy for me to try to surrender. In fact, it's been horribly hard. I'm one of the original Puritans. If I'm not working hard, I think I'm committing a terrible sin. And I want to put people down so bad and impress them with my accomplishments and build myself up in my own eyes. So I'm constantly asking of everything I do, "Hey, where will that get you? Why are you doing this?" When I don't have good, specific answers to these questions inside myself, I feel terribly uneasy. I feel that if someone found out I wasn't working toward some specific accomplishment, it would surely go bad for me in some way or other.

One evening recently, I was looking around for something productive to do and it was such a relief when I had the thought, "You don't need to do anything. You've done your day's work. What would you like to do tonight?" So I very happily took a nice, hot bath and went to bed to read a horse magazine. What a delicious feeling.

While I do many things I enjoy, it isn't often that I do them without feeling a little guilty. Yet my work is always pretty well done up and things are in pretty good order so there is no reason for feeling guilty. But I do.

It is one thing for me to say I know I should surrender to life. It is another thing, and a much harder one, to feel comfortable with the idea. Yet, looking back I can see that almost all the good in my life came out of surrender.

And almost all the bad feelings and bad times came out of overcontrolling things. Despite those great experiences with surrender, though, it is still terribly hard to handle my feelings. And it is so hard to listen to God's voice telling me to do what's best for right now as well as I can see it, instead of that Puritan voice in me that tells me I must use every minute for profitable, constructive tasks that result in accomplishments that show and that make me look big in my eyes and the eyes of my fellow man.

I grant you I don't hear those voices quite that clearly. I think I'm still sane. But I do believe in a God that speaks to me if I will only listen fairly carefully.

One night this past spring Jackie and I were wrestling with the decision whether to teach half time at half-time pay, or not. Later in bed, Jackie asked me, "Have you talked to God about this, Jess? What does He say?"

I had recently been reading some Vince Lombardi stories and they prompted me to say to my wife, "Yes, I asked God what I should do and He said, 'You know best, my son.' " In a way that's funny. In another way it sounds terrible, and yet in even another way it is true. There is a God to whom we can relate as a loving father instead of looking at that same God as we would our jailer, our torturer, and our judge.

My AA friend, Vince, calls that latter view of God "Grandma's God." He says we have to get rid of our frightening view of Grandma's God and get one that really works in our lives. I believe what he says because he lives the kind of life filled with kindness and gentleness that the Bible asks for, where you can tell he is a Christian by the loving way he acts toward his brothers.

I needed the idea of surrender when I came back to school in the fall after my cancer scare. I was faced with a problem for my teaching. The way I handled it is one of the best examples I can give you of the idea of surrender and how I was trying to use this in all areas of my life.

Before I had been teaching my ideas to one large group

of students and then meeting with them in small discussion groups. In my lectures I was very concerned to make sure I talked about certain topics like acceptance and the Zulu story in a certain way and in a certain order. I had seen that those things worked for me before and I was afraid to get away from them.

But that fall I had three different classes instead of one all on the same course. I was worried how I could possibly cover my material in my way with an opportunity for class participation and still keep track of where I was in the three different classes.

Luckily, the spring before, Gerry Sullivan had given me a book on Zen to read. Through the book, Gerry showed me that there is no way I can say truth about life because all statements about life are just statements and not life. You could tell someone about a rose or a sunset for a week and they would still be amazed when they saw their first rose or sunset. I could talk about life and be kind of close, but I would still be wrong. Everything I said would be a contradiction with something else. The truth would always be somewhere in between. So I saw that when we listen to someone we must listen in between the lines because that's where the truth is, in between the lines.

I went into my three classes and tried to teach each of them the same way I had the previous year. But after a few hours with each class I saw how different they were so I cut loose from my plans and tried to surrender. I talked to each one about what seemed most important to them or me at that minute. The funny thing that happened was that I covered the same material I had covered before. And I got the same things across to each of my three classes, even though I covered very different things with each of them. And I didn't have to make any effort to keep track of what I had covered with each group or when. It all came out and the reason it did was the thing Gerry Sullivan had taught me. The truth was in between the lines. The truth of me was in me. There were no problems organizing that. And there was no way of hiding me even if I tried.

As I wrote the previous two paragraphs I had an insight into something that I think made a big difference in my students' reaction to me. Before the cancer scare I was the powerful person sitting up in the front of the room. My big teacher voice made me sound to some like the Messiah who knew all. That way they couldn't help but be disappointed. And they couldn't help coming at me in funny ways. But once I sat down in that circle of chairs with my students, it was very clear to them how confused I was. So we set to work on our own problems as much as we could. Sometimes we needed a distraction so we picked on someone else and created an uproar. But often we managed to work softly and sweetly on our own problems and some very nice things happened. Other times we didn't know what to do so we just sat and stared at each other.

Don't think that isn't an awful feeling. Here I was, the big Ph.D. in psychology, and I already had my first book and lots of triumphs behind me. But I didn't know what to do or what to say. I was so frightened at the chaos I thought of going back to lecturing. But I had done that and it wasn't what I was looking for. So all I could do was face my failure of the moment, my confusion and the chaos I saw in that room.

Was that really me sitting there speechless? Yes. Couldn't I think of anything better to do than what I was doing? No. So that was reality for me then. It gave me awful feelings of futility and fear to see that reality.

It's the same when someone dies. You go to their loved ones and you can't think of anything great to say. But you go and say, "I'm sorry," and whatever else seems appropriate and you settle for that. It isn't much, but it's all you've got.

I know in my head that I have to accept that reality, but my feelings keep screaming, "You're a big phony

dope. Other people know what to say and do in situations
like this and you should, too."

If there is one thing that I would say is the guts of this
book, it is my attempt to see the reality of the moment as
clearly and honestly as I humanly can.

When I try to work on a false view of reality with a
false, exaggerated view of what I am, and when I am
concerned about what I should be, I can do nothing because I am nothing.

But when I try to face reality as well as I can dimly see
it with my weak self just as I am, I can do something.
And no matter how little it is, that something is gloriously
better than nothing.

So these are the stormy feelings that come out of trying
to surrender. There seems to be a frightening powerless-
ness in it. But there is the greatest power at my command
in it.

By surrender, as I used the word, I mean to surrender
to what I really am. No deals. No "wouldn't it be nice if?"
Just surrender to what really is. Sure I can't ever know
reality exactly and that scares me. But I can see enough
of it so that I can deal with it—and get better at dealing
with it.

I can't tell you how strange it feels and how hard it is
to turn my back on a conventional way of teaching and
dealing with situations using structures that I know work.
All I have to guide me is the feeling there might be a better way. Even with all the deep emotional rewards I have
received during the past three years from my work and
my writing, I am still terribly shaken by deep doubts.

I hope I can find the courage to go on as I have. It
would be very misleading if you felt that I was doing
something like this easily. You might feel that the difficulties you are having are a sign something is wrong with
you. It isn't that. It's a sign you are working and making
some hard choices.

There are a thousand ways I can run away from myself

and there is only one way of facing myself. Those are bad odds. And my temptation is to slip. So I struggle each day to avoid going crazy. Not mental institution crazy, but crazy in the sense Old Lodge Skins speaks of it in the book *Little Big Man.*

Little Big Man and Old Lodge Skins came to a Cheyenne village that had been burned by the white men with the women and children killed. Little Big Man asked, "Grandfather, why do the white men fight this way?"

Said Old Lodge Skins, "The white man is crazy. He does not know where the center of the earth is."

That's the kind of crazy I mean. I can go crazy frequently during a day by cutting up people with mean words, killing people with my eyes, expecting people to be the way I want them to be, punishing them when they won't oblige, and constantly judging everyone and everything. How can I know what anyone should do when I am so desperately needing and asking guidance for myself?

So many people make that mistake of thinking that because I can talk of these things I can do them. I can't do them. I'm struggling as hard as I can to try to do them. It is so hard trying to be honest and live out in the open. It is so hard to love. And because I am so afraid to love—you are alone.

When you have trouble doing these things I talk about, don't worry. It is a sign you're alive, not that you're weak or a failure.

Teaching is so much of my life right now. That's why I can give you a better idea of what I am doing by talking of my life in the classroom. I'm trying to do the same things outside the classroom but they aren't as easy for me to communicate to you.

There are about a hundred classrooms on our campus. I haven't found but two that are set up for real discussion around a square or circle so everybody can see everybody else. How can you have a real discussion unless you can see the faces? And unless you can put up name signs so the faces have names?

I find I can get this effect by having my students move their chairs into a circle and having each student make a folded paper sign with his name on it. At the end of the hour we put our chairs back in order.

I've found other things, too. Earlier in my teaching the title "Dr." seemed to become a barrier between some of my students and me as closer relationships developed. I now encourage my students to call me whatever name they are most comfortable with. I also found that as our group got closer to each other there was a desire on the part of the group to express their unity. So we came to hold hands in the circle at the beginning and end of each hour. Some of my students just hold hands perfunctorily and a few even hate it. But most of my students and I find it a very helpful thing.

While there is touching and the special language of touching involved, that isn't so much the point as is the message of our unity that we send each other.

For the last two and one half years I have been sitting in groups like that for two or three hours a day. I have found out many things about myself. Much of it I have been able to incorporate into my life outside those rooms. Many of the things I have seen in those rooms I have never seen written down. Many of the problems I have run into in those rooms have never been told of.

A couple of my teacher friends have found similar problems in their rooms. All I can say is that something is wrong. Many people who write about trying to run a human classroom don't tell about having problems with their students. Yet the teachers I believe in find that not all students welcome openness. Some resent it and fight it bitterly. So something is wrong. Either my friends and I are doing something wrong to cause the resistance we find or the other people writing about their classrooms aren't reporting their problems. I also find that when I tell my fine fellow teachers of one of my recent failures in my classroom, they usually are relieved to hear of my mistake and tell me of some mistake they just made but were afraid to tell anyone about. So one day soon I'm going to write a book titled *How I Fail as a Teacher—Each Day*.

I think the unwillingness I see in us as teachers to speak of our failures is a good example of how fear of our feelings works to create a great gap between me and you. When I deny giving you my feelings about me, I mislead you. You think I'm supercool. So out of fear you act supercool, too. And we end up lying to each other and feeling alone and separated.

You see what a bad thing I do in God's eyes when I deny my human imperfect and try to make you think I'm perfect like God? What a terrible way for me to treat my brother. And do you see what a good thing I do when as much as I can, I reveal my human imperfections? You can see that you are not alone in your human imperfections. If there are two of us weirdos—you and me—then there is hope that there are others around us and we just have to find and make contact with our separated brethren.

But do you see what many of the educational reformers are telling you and me that hurts us so? They are telling us we should be good teachers and good parents. They imply it is easy. They imply that they are doing a great job, and worst of all, they imply that we aren't doing what we should because we are stupid or contrary or both. Now I think that's an awful thing they are saying to you and me.

Why won't those reformers speak of their failures in a deep and specific way? I know they can't help but fail some because they are human. So they either have to run and hide from their failures and deny them or they have to lie openly by refusing to admit those failures.

I have talked to many teachers who are doing what the reformers ask. Yet, when I tell these teachers of my problems and my failures, most of them tell me back

about theirs and each of us finds real comfort in the
knowledge that we are not alone. We know we are doing
a pretty good job. But it isn't perfect. The knowledge that
other people are finding the same problems shows us we
are not all screwed up like the silence of the reformers
suggests.

Rather than face the music about his own reality, I see
that the reformer frequently blames someone else for the
problem. If a kid talks back to him he blames the problem on the parents, the police, society, or the previous
teachers. While all these causes operate, I find my students can pretty well shift gears from one class hour to
the next and change from demons to angels and back to
demons.

An awful lot of the trouble I see in my room is a result
of what I have done five minutes or five days earlier and
it is coming back to me. I find I pay for my mistakes right
now. And most of what I pay for are my mistakes, not
someone else's.

I see a great lawfulness in life. In the classroom I find
the first law is "Bug and thou shalt be bugged in return."
When I hurt a student I get hurt back. So I see the wisdom of Vince when he says that AA teaches him the laws
of life and how to live in harmony with those laws by
surrendering to them and to the Higher Power that's
manifest in those laws. And we need to do all this so
smoothly that there's no odor of sanctity about us.

Pope John had thick leather soles put on his fancy red
shoes so he could walk around Rome and see his people.
He went into the jails, not because it was the saintly or
the crowd-pleasing thing to do, but because he wanted to
see those people, too, and they couldn't come to see him.
His saintliness was tucked away inside him where it
worked in his life instead of outside him like a cloak. Because of it, John left a deep impression on the whole
Christian and non-Christian world.

I would like to write my book about my failures as a

teacher and some of the problems I find in the classroom because that's reality as I see it. Those teachers and parents who are troubled by their shortcomings as I am by mine will enjoy meeting a fellow sufferer. And right now that book seems like one of the two things I want to do next.

As I said earlier, I see these same struggles going on in the rest of my life. Facing death as I did perhaps had some good effects. I mentioned earlier the line in the book *Little Big Man* where Little Big Man wakes up after Custer's last battle and realizes he wasn't killed in the battle. He says, "When you should have died and didn't you ain't ever the same." I have said that in so many of my classes. I like whatever kind of day we are having because I know it beats hell out of the alternative of not having that day.

There's a bad side to being too scared and that is, I can be way too frantic at times. But I find some of that frantic grasping at life is leaving me.

So what have I been doing outside of class that's like what's in class? Well, I've been trying to take the days and moments as they come and do what feels like the best thing to do at the moment, even if I can't always figure out why.

I've seen that I've got some good new relationships and some stronger old ones. But not without some pain. I don't find this path I'm on to be the lovely pink cloud so many describe. To me the agony comes when I see I'm in a relationship and I'm screwing up. Or, something is needed in that situation that I don't have.

This morning, as I was writing these pages, one of my closest friends was telling me of his troubles. I was listening to him and saying a few things. But I had the awful feeling I was adding to his problems instead of being any comfort or help to him as he has so often been to me. I find it's hard to face shortcomings like that in one of my closest relationships. I find myself saying, "Is that all there is to you, Jess Lair?" And I have to answer, "Yes, that's all there is so far." So often I wish there was so much more.

Some of the friends I had made earlier left the university and there has been no more communication between us. This told me a sad thing about how little there really was in the relationship on each of our parts and especially mine. Some of my other friends and I found that our relationships just didn't grow past a certain point. Again, that told me some troubling things about me that I tried to accept for the truths that they were. Gerry Sullivan had been a friend before but we found more and more things we wanted to talk about so we went to coffee together more frequently and became much closer friends.

When I first came to Bozeman I tried to have instant friendships with the businessmen downtown. I thought that since I had been a businessman for fifteen years and a professor for only five years I shouldn't get caught in a college versus businessmen split. But I was.

No matter how long I had been a businessman, I was now a professor and I scared people and brought out their prejudices. So I heard remarks about "people with their noses in the government trough." I got the feeling from some that I was a parasite taking lots of money for nothing. I learned I couldn't push friendships downtown.

Three years later I found the problem had solved itself. I had found a number of businessmen who needed me and who looked forward to seeing me.

About two or three years ago I got a clearer sense of an idea that has become of central importance to me. That was my need for other people. I had seen my need for others not too long after my heart attack. But my participation in Emotions Anonymous and teaching helped me see the idea of my need for others far more clearly and sharply than ever before.

My students were constantly telling me how they wanted to help people. I objected to that idea. My objections grew stronger and stronger as I saw more clearly how often my students were using the idea of helping someone as a way to put themselves above someone or to separate themselves from others. And my students were so hesitant to give what was most needed to their brother. They didn't want to give of themselves. They would give their time, or their goods, even their money, but they didn't want to give what was most needed—part of themselves. Particularly needed by their brother was some sense of their own human imperfection so that their imperfect brother would not feel like the only one who was imperfect because no one else would speak of their imperfection to him.

I didn't have much success getting this idea across to my students. They were so sold on the idea of helping others only in a surface, material way and they needed the idea so much they couldn't give it up.

But I benefited because I came to see my own need for other people much more clearly. Now I compromise with my students by agreeing with them that it is okay to help others, if you admit it is because you need them much more than they need your money or goods. The giver should be grateful.

So I was saying to all the people I was in contact with, "I need you." I found many ways to say it.

One group I said it to was fifty Bozeman businessmen. I was asked to speak to them on human relations. I accepted the speech, but as the time drew near to speak I realized I was in trouble. I had a bad heart toward Bozeman businessmen because of the way some of them had treated me when I came to town. I told myself not to be foolish. These weren't the same people. That helped, but not much. I also worked at keeping myself as rested and as calm as possible for the whole week ahead of my speech because when I get overtired I'm much more likely to do some dumb thing.

I even turned down a sure-fire chance to shoot an elk

the day before my speech because I knew how tired I could get from hunting and decided the elk would have to wait.

So I walked into my speech fairly calm, rested, and relaxed. I got a warm introduction from a good friend, Chuck Lein, and I got lucky. I stuck to my own story and told how I had blown some crucial human relations problems and why. I told them just how I was trying to learn from my mistakes and what my present successes and failures were. And I told them that I was speaking to them not just for the money but because I needed them. And I asked them to consider their need for their employees.

It was one of the most rewarding speeches I ever made. Because I came at them soft and sweet, I got to see the soft and sweet side of every one of those fifty businessmen. My students in our college town figure that no businessman in town has a heart at all, to say nothing of a soft, sweet heart. But my students weren't there that evening and I was.

So I was able to speak to this group and others of my need for them. Did I need all of them? No. Only those who chose to need me back, those who were on my wave length. But that was enough people to fill my cup up much more than it had ever been filled before.

Perhaps I am much more an external person than I should be. In the past, too often, I had sacrificed my family's interest when it had interfered with an outside interest. But now I was able to work at that problem from both ways. As I found lots of real love and respect for me from people outside the family I was freer to do those things with and for my family that I had never been able to do because of all the outside forces pulling on me.

During these past two and one half years, I have been much more of a help to my wife in furnishing thought and leadership in the family. And I have been able to be closer to my wife. We have found many of our older family problems are clearing themselves up and getting easier to handle. Also, because we aren't creating so many new problems, there seem to be fewer problems around. Now we in the family can spend more time enjoying ourselves when we are together instead of WORKING ON EACH OTHER'S PROBLEMS. That's nicer, too.

I've studied Vince Lombardi very carefully and I have all the books written on him. He had one idea that I think might have been basic to him. I know it is vital to me. Lombardi's priorities were, in order: 1. his God; 2. his family; and 3. the Green Bay Packers.

I'm sure Lombardi would have been the first to admit that occasionally he got his priorities mixed up a little. But they were his priorities. His life tells me he tried to live by them and it doesn't look to me as if he left behind an embittered wife and family because of putting his family last.

Lombardi's priorities are my priorities, too, and while I'm sure I get them mixed up in more ways than Lombardi ever thought of, I'm trying to hold to them.

I mentioned the word "surrender" at the beginning of the chapter. That sounds like a simple idea, but it isn't. It's one of the biggest paradoxes I know of. Surrender means giving up, relaxing, floating with life. But the act of surrendering is a conscious, cold-blooded, deliberate act. It is a very unsurrendering thing to do, the deliberate act of surrender. So I don't understand the paradox, but I'm trying to surrender anyway.

I watch my friend Vince, the AA member of twenty-five years, and he has surrendered so well and to such an extent he is the sweetest human I know. His example encourages me.

I used to be the biggest writer of plans in the world and now I don't have any beyond the fact that I will probably teach half time again next quarter and finish this book. These are the two things I'm doing now, but in general, there is nothing that I'm trying to do. Yet I get nearly everything done. I don't think about results yet the days are packed with what I used to call accomplishments but now see as simply side effects of living.

The best explanation of surrender I have found is the comparison to a car ride. We get in this car on the passenger's side and sit back. No one is visible in the driver's seat yet the car starts up and moves out. Some of the time I can stay in the passenger's seat even though it takes great effort. But there are so many times when I jump into the driver's seat because I've got a better idea where my car should go than my Higher Power.

When I surrender and sit in the passenger seat, I am turning my will and my life over to the care of God as each of us understands Him. What is so puzzling to me is why I am so anxious to hang onto my old ways or to take them back. What good are they? It was those old ways that gave me my heart attack. My new way has kept me alive and reasonably sane. Yet I am horrified to see how frequently I try to grab back my old ways and get into the driver's seat.

As a result of these eleven years since my heart attack, I now have a clear view of what can be ahead for me— abundant living. I didn't think such a thing was possible on this earth. I felt that for imperfect human beings life would inevitably consist of lots of grief, sorrows, and suffering. But I have seen some people who live abundantly and joyously. They face their sorrows with serenity. And because they cause so few of their own sorrows, they have fewer sorrows to face.

I see abundant living as coming out of learning the great laws of life and living in harmony with those laws. I see abundant living as coming from having a spiritual awakening that pierces our conscious and subconscious mind right to the depth of our being that frees us from our conflicts and doubt. I see abundant living as turning our will and our lives over to the care of God as each of us understands Him—surrender.

It's that simple. It isn't easy but it is simple. And it can be done. I have seen people do it. We can live in abundance and in serenity.

As I see it, the secret of abundant living is seeing my need for my Higher Power and my need for mutual relationships—what we call Mutual Need Therapy. That is the other book I will probably be working on soon. The title would express what to me is one of my central predicaments—*Because I Am Afraid to Love, You Are Alone.*

14

Jackie

Now I am in the present. I am sitting in our camping trailer parked beside our new log home up Bridger Canyon.

I look out the window at our horses eating the brown August grass. The sky is blue and then gray with low, scudding clouds that foretell winter.

The mountains are bare of snow, but in a few weeks' time they will be white with the early September snows.

I ask myself, "What has all of this meant to me? Am I a different person because of this life I have led and must continue to lead? Is there any meaning in all of this?"

To answer the last question first, I would tend to say "No." I have learned to stop looking for meaning. I have learned to stop asking "Why?"

It is foolish to ask questions that have no answer. My job is to accept and to grow. I have learned that unless I accept what life has to offer me, and learn from it, I will surely die.

I know I am a different person. A better person, I do believe.

I have found in the past two years a deeper, firmer belief in God.

In my delayed adolescence period, which lasted for a very long time, I had lost most of my childhood religious beliefs. I now have found a deep and lasting religious belief. One that still fits very well with the faith of my childhood.

I used to say that religion was for well people. I still believe this. Since the death of Jesus Christ over nineteen hundred years ago, I do not believe that there has been a mortal alive who truly can comfort the afflicted. In the presence of illness and death we are all so mortally alone.

As you might have guessed, I wrestle nightly with thoughts of death. I am still fearful. I have entertained thoughts of my own death, too. This partly because of Jess's illnesses and partly because I am forty-two years old and have begun to realize that my own life will not go on forever.

I had felt close to death in my early twenties when I had two spinal fusions in the space of two weeks, one fusion not having fused properly. My attitude was simpler then because I had not lived as yet.

Is there a Heaven? Is there a Hell? I believe so. My belief, for those who care to know, is that we make our Heaven and our Hell here on earth. Death brings an extension of that. If we have found true serenity here on earth, we will have serenity for eternity. The opposite is also true.

I have found in the twelve steps of Emotions Anonymous and/or Alcoholics Anonymous my rules for living. Through practice of these steps, day by day, I progress toward peace and serenity.

I found that I was not satisfied with just giving up neurotic behavior. I had to go beyond the giving up and find the peace and serenity that is there as a gift from God.

I found that there is no peace and serenity without a Higher Power. I guess you could say that I found religion. I am grateful.

To answer the second question, I think I am different. Many people have remarked as much to me. My brother John even asked at one point what had caused me to change. I hope John will read this book someday. Then he will better understand.

I am now in the process of learning to "let go." I am at an age when my children are starting to remove themselves from my life. This process is never easy, but I find that it is especially hard where we have all been so very close because of the incidents in our lives.

Our children, too, are finding this hard. In recent years we have seen a daughter marry and a son build his own home and set off to college. They are having as hard a time letting go of us as we are them.

They are fiercely independent, and want no advice or help. But they also want to come back into our lives whenever they feel a need, and completely on their own terms.

Needless to say, this causes friction. We are working on finding a way. We have tried at least a half-dozen ways so far, all more or less unsuccessful.

Some days I am lonely for them. Then other days I do not care to see them. And so we go. I am sure we will all weather this period in our lives. Our parents did before us, and their parents before them.

Now to the first question. What has all of this meant to me?

I view this question with dismay. My feelings are mixed. My answer will be slow in coming.

In the two years since the cancer scare, life has been mixed with sorrows and joys as all life must ever be.

Jess's recovery was not as smooth as I would have liked. We had to make a third trip to Minneapolis in the year 1970. Jess was reacting poorly to a medication. But we did not know that. He was overly tired that fall. I attributed this to the traumatic spring and early summer. As fall wore on, two students came to me on separate occasions and remarked that they were worried about him. He was forgetful. He slurred his words. He fell asleep in his chair. I cut his medication down to one pill a day. He still continued this pattern of behavior.

By this time we were too uneasy to trust in our Bozeman physician alone. He, kind man that he is, recognized this and suggested that we again return to Minneapolis.

Jess entered St. Mary's for the third time. It was the medication. He was stepped up to four pills a day again and zonked out on the doctors. They pulled his medicine and he was himself in a few days. Examined from stem to stern, he received a clean bill of health. I was to take him home the next day. That night Jess celebrated in his hospital room with some cronies. He was debilitated from many enemas and other indignities required for tests. His friends left. Jess slept. He awoke feeling sick. He went into the bathroom. He fell, he had little pulse, hardly any heartbeat. A resident was summoned. From the hard cider the resident smelled it was a toss-up between dead drunk or almost dead from other causes. The resident, not knowing Jess, voted for dead drunk. Dr. Mazzitello arrived. He knew Jess was not a drinking man.

He explained to me later that Jess's heart had stopped for a short while and then resumed beating.

This incident has been repeated three times in the past two years. It is very frightening to witness. Jess becomes gray, completely soaked in perspiration, and barely conscious. Each time he has recovered before help arrives. I do not recover quite so easily.

In the past two years I have entered my forties. My hair has become streaked with gray. My teeth are going, one by one. I looked in the mirror one day and realized that my face was falling. I torture myself by pulling upward just in front of my ears. As the skin goes taut I look ten years younger. I wish I were rich enough for a face-lift. Lord knows I'm vain enough.

Over twenty years ago Jess and I once stayed on an island in Lake Vermilion in northern Minnesota. On that island was a log cabin built with a view on two sides. We had a dream of someday building a home like that.

When the finality of certain death was lifted, two years ago, Jess and I both decided to enjoy each day just a little more. The next spring, with the help of a publisher's advance, some savings, and some cash values in our life insurance, we stripped ourselves to the bone and bought some acreage in Bridger Canyon. An artist named Cliff Fulker began to build our log home.

Cliff would not have liked being called an artist. He was a real Montana man, a hard-living, happy Montana cowboy turned carpenter. With no help from our plans or our contractor, Cliff built us a beautiful, warm, lovely home. He built it with love and respect for the wood and us. Our home became one of Cliff's masterpieces.

On the final day, as Cliff smoothed the cement walk in front of our home, we took a stick and wrote his name. He will always be a part of our home, as truly as Picasso is a part of his masterpieces no matter who owns them.

This past winter we put up yards and yards of snow fence to keep the snows at bay. Jess built a $350 barn that cost over $1,200 in lumber alone. (Jess told me the barn would cost only $350. I foolishly believed him. I think he said this merely to calm my money nerves. He is not foolish enough to have believed the smaller sum.)

Jess and the family skied. I was too fat to get up once I fell. I stayed home and ate.

The peace and strength I had found the past two years was at low ebb. I realized this and determined to get back on my own what God had given me freely in crisis.

This past March, 1972, Jess once again had a "heart stopper" in the bathroom. It was on my birthday. He was tense and overtired. Discouraged with school, he was depressed.

Depression is a red flag to me. I always expect trouble when Jess is down in the dumps.

Jess had gone into the bedroom for a cat nap earlier in the evening. He got up, felt ill, walked into the bathroom, and slumped over.

Again the gray color, the horrendous perspiring, the nausea. I called our doctor.

Jess, Jr., and I took him to the hospital. He looked well by the time we arrived. He stayed in the hospital for three days resting.

The winter quarter was almost ended. Others took Jess's classes. Jess was to rest until the end of March.

At this time Jess, Jr., began to see what was happening in his own life. He came to me quite sadly one evening and sat down for a long talk about his father.

I can best summarize this talk by saying that our nineteen-year-old son began to let go of his father and me.

He, rightly, said that he had to let go of us, and that when the time came for his father to die, well, he would have to die.

"I can no longer live on this tightrope of fear. If the old man is going to die, he's just going to have to die. I have to begin living my own life. I can't be torn up any more," he said.

I heard my son's words with relief. He is too young to spend so much time worrying about his father. Jess, Jr., took his first step toward letting God run his life. He feels some guilt and anxiety over the mixed feelings he has toward us and our traumas, but a doctor friend of ours summed Jess, Jr., up quite well when he said, "Little Jess is a cool head. He's getting his life together. He may have some problems, but they'll be no worse than anyone else has."

Jess and I were supposed to fly to Santa Rosa, California, the end of March, where Jess was to speak for two days. We contemplated canceling. We decided not to. We would take a leisurely drive out and vacation on the way. We needed a break. We had not left the children for any reason but health for over ten years. They needed a break from us also.

The trip was delightful and in our usual fashion we shared each other's thoughts all the way out and back. We "joyed" in each other's presence. It was a good trip.

Jess had some problems with blacking out a year ago this summer. We have decided that he must go half time at the university for this next year. We will have to pull in our belts again. We have done it before, and we are not afraid.

The future is beyond our control. In a few weeks we are going to drive to Minneapolis so that Jess can have a checkup. Worry is present, but not crippling.

On the other hand, Jess has moments when he feels faint and weak. He has something wrong with his throat, he chokes on food once, twice, sometimes a dozen times a day. As I sit here writing, he chokes across from me on a little raisin. In my usual fashion I look up and say, "You have to see the doctor about that, I don't relish sticking a knife in your throat so that you can have an air hole."

Like Tevye in *Fiddler on the Roof,* I also say, "On the other hand . . ." On the other hand, Jess looks well. His color is good. He is not as tired as he was last week at the end of summer session. At the present time I feel optimistic.

I find that the most difficult part is to train oneself to live always in the present. At first I thought I couldn't learn to live only in the present. I must have goals. I must know where I am going.

I must answer myself: For the past forty-two years I have spent most of my life either looking backward at the past or forward to the future. My mind has been smothered beneath plans for myself, my husband, and my children.

None of these plans have borne fruit, and the future has always brought to my doorstep an untold abundance of things I could not have dreamed of.

As for the past, I have a very selective memory. I remember truth as only I saw it. Haven't you often found yourself telling of an incident from your childhood to someone who was there, only to find that his memory of it differs drastically from yours?

So, the past is a mystery also, for how do we know what is the truth?

The present is here and now and I find I must live in it only.

Am I being an ostrich? I do not believe so. My finite mind can only deal with one thing at a time. And I choose the present. I believe we all must make that choice sooner or later in our lives.

Another fact I have found to be true these past few years is that our herculean efforts to be open to life and to work ceaselessly at problem solving have had a momentous side benefit.

That benefit is that my anger is mostly gone. You know that anger that seems to be in most of us at birth? That uncertain tension that causes most of us to flare up at odd moments? That ungoverned part of us that lies deep with in and that rears its foreign nature at we know not what or when?

I can remember, as a teen-ager, being so full of anger and tension that I would wake up in the morning with a knot in my stomach. I oftentimes made life a living hell for my younger sister by many cruelties.

One that stands out in my mind was staring at her while she ate her breakfast because hearing her chew infuriated me. I would make my younger sister literally choke on her food with the seething anger that would spill out in her presence. I didn't hate that dear little girl. I was just hateful to the world, and she was the victim all too often.

This is the kind of anger I mean. The nonsensical, misdirected anger that so often hurts the innocent. I feel it rarely now. There is not much need.

I used to blame my parents, my teachers, my husband, or my children for this anger. Now I see it is not so much a matter of blaming. I see this type of anger as an almost universal separateness that is in so many of us. It is caused more by an "absence of" than "because of."

And the funny thing is that I found that I have to empty myself consciously in order to control this anger. I have a constant prayer that I send up to God. I simply say, "Empty me, Lord."

I find that these words are an excellent way for me to control not only anger, but jealousy, resentments, and all of the other character defects I have.

How many of you are shy? I suffer mightily from shyness. My shyness has caused me to be a non-joiner. I become angry and tense in a crowd, purely because I am shy.

I rarely ask anyone over to my house. I find it hard to go to very many people's homes also. Having left all of my childhood and young adult associations behind five years ago has left me feeling quite lonely sometimes.

I sometimes worry that I am not more sociable. I worry that I will have a lonely life should Jess finally be defeated in his duel with death. But, for now, I am willing to push aside my fears in the enjoyment that we two share in our daily intense encounters with each other.

For most of the past twenty-three years we have completely filled each other's needs for other people. We have been a society of two. I will trust that the fulfillment this has brought me will suffice in the years to come.

These few instances when the dragon contained within will arise are few indeed compared to the many years when anger bubbled to the surface daily, and at the most meager provocation.

As I have come closer to my Higher Power, and He has begun to rule my heart and my emotions, each day is filled with a new peace. I recognize this peace as a gift from God, one that I have worked for, and must work to keep. This grace is not showered upon us as manna from heaven. This wonderful gift of peace comes to me from living and working the twelve steps of Emotions Anonymous.

I recently learned a beautiful lesson in making amends (step nine of the EA steps).

Our son bought some new ski boots. The kind that must be foamed to fit the foot. He could not find a time to get them foamed that fit his schedule and that of the store where he made his purchase. He complained to me about it several times. Then he solved his problem without telling me.

I had occasion to go to the offending (or so I thought) store. I asked in irate tones for an appointment to foam my son's boots. I threw the owners of the store into a tizzy and an appointment was made for the following day.

To my shame, that evening as I told my son that he had an appointment to get his boots foamed, he informed me that he had solved the problem. "And furthermore," he asked me, "what are you doing butting into my business and causing trouble?"

The old Jackie would have dropped the subject and allowed the discomfort to keep me out of that store. The new me called the owner that very night and apologized. The lovely lady was most gracious, and no doubt surprised, and now there is a bond between us.

A small thing, yes, but put on a daily basis, making immediate, truthful amends for wrongdoing has given me many rewards. And most important, it gives me that wonderful feeling of serenity that I prize above most everything.

Of course, making amends to a storekeeper is easier than to one's own family, I am afraid. The everyday angers that arise from close relationships are of a more intense variety. But, here too, I find that I must do it. If I do not, all too often the way is then opened for self-pity and resentment. And they are real stiflers of serenity.

Webster's dictionary says the word "serene" means "marked by utter calm." Another definition that I like is "clear and free of storms or unpleasant change." The latter definition refers to the skies or the sea. And yet, we can all see that it can refer to our own private depths as well.

I find that much of my serenity comes from really believing the famous Serenity Prayer.

> God, grant me the serenity
> To accept the things I cannot change;
> Courage to change the things I can;
> And the wisdom to know the difference.

I find a great deal of truth and wisdom in the books of Catherine Marshall as well. I especially read and reread *To Live Again* and *Beyond Ourselves*.

Reading and contemplation are a daily need to me. I must have a quiet hour to myself each and every day in order to examine my life and my mental and emotional growth. If I miss as little as one day, I find a little difficulty arising the next day.

As a youngster I remember hearing about the requirement that every Catholic priest in the world must read his daily office. This was a duty that was required daily of these men of God. As a young person I was horrified at the thought of having to read the same thing each day of one's life.

I do not know if this reading of the divine office is still a requirement of the priesthood or not. But some form of it most certainly must be. We finite human beings need a conscious contact with the God of our understanding each and every day. Without it peace and serenity are impossible.

Many times when Jess and I have traveled, troubled, lonely people have come to us for help and understanding. We have so little to offer them. It is hard to say, "You must go and seek your own help. Our peace cannot be your peace." It is sad to think that I cannot even give my own family what I have found. Each and every one of us is alone in this. There is one guarantee I can give, however. If you are willing to say to yourself, "I want peace of mind and serenity at any price," you will find it. The price is oftentimes high. The road is an agony to travel many times. But, dear reader, it is there for every living person.

There is joy in reaching for this goal, also. I oftentimes have thought that without my earthy sense of humor, my God-given ability to laugh at myself, I would go insane. One of my husband's favorite quotes comes from I know not where. It is this: "Anyone who can look at his own feet and not laugh has either no sense of humor or no sense of proportion."

I extend this quote and say: "Anyone who can look at his own *life* and not laugh has either no sense of humor or no sense of proportion." God save me from the humorless.

At our local church there is a young priest who makes me grin every time he steps up to say Mass. He is bursting with youth and wry humor, and his offering of daily Mass must certainly bring a smile to God's face each day. He is a happy young man, full of life and plans. I smile through his every Mass. How blessed is a man who can make others smile.

Many times my humor in the privacy of our home is quite broad. My children protest—"Mother, you're gross." But many times I feel that I am teaching them to laugh at things that should be laughed at instead of treated with a false reverence.

I must tell a story about one of my sons here. I won't mention his name for obvious reasons.

The day for sex education had arrived at our local school. A local doctor gave a talk and then asked for questions. My son's group of sixth-grade boys had many questions about girls' breasts. Finally the harassed doctor said, "I don't see why you boys are so interested in breasts. They are only fatty tissue." As our son told us at dinner that night, "At recess, after the doctor talked, this girl knocked me down on the playground and stepped on my jewels. I told her, Robin, if you don't get your foot off of my jewels, I'll kick you in your fat."

I am happy our sons can speak with us of incidents of this sort. And more important, that we all laughed at their hyperreaction after a tense sex lecture at school.

Another fact I have discovered is that I no longer believe that we can do whatever we want, and be with any person. I have become selective of my environment. I believe we control our lives by controlling our environment.

Since I was a very small child, I have been most serene when alone. Drawing, listening to music, writing. All of these things have always brought me peace.

Contrary to my nature, as a young married I was constantly pulled into social functions.

How many of us really enjoy rounds of parties? How many of us really enjoy the ever present daily fallacy that we must be with people and "living it up"?

I love my family. I enjoy a very small group of people with whom I am in tune. I love them more now that I am me.

I have learned the joy of being myself.

I guess I have to try to be really truthful here.

Previously I said "I guess I got religion." That was a quibble. What I really mean is this.

Off and on over my entire adult life I have been overcome by my neurosis. I can lay my behavior at the doorstep of my handicapped child, having too many children too fast, my husband's health, or whether the rhubarb had enough rain. But, boiled down to the nitty-gritty, I was and am an emotionally immature person.

I received the best of psychiatry for my ills, and I would be first in line to pin a medal on two of the three psychiatrists I have seen. But I remained dependent upon psychiatry *until* I came into Emotions Anonymous. And here and now I must admit that with the aid of my Higher Power (as I understand Him) I had a spiritual experience that has changed my life.

No, dear friends who might wonder, Jesus Christ did not come and speak to me in a grand and glorious vision. But, for the first time, seven years ago I came to believe in something outside of myself. That something was God, to me. I had always had my childish belief in God, but what I speak of here is a mature faith in Him, with the spiritual awakening which then occurs.

My thinking, my awareness, my physical self have undergone a change that has stood the only test I understand. I have been a different person for seven years now. I have been a person I could finally stand to live with. And that, to me, is good mental health.

Though I have had this gift from God for seven years now I know that I could lose it today if I take my eye from the source of this gift. In order to remain as near to mental health as I can, I had to come to a rather startling conclusion about myself. I had to face that for me, my mental health could only be maintained a day at a time, and that I would have to work on it until two days after I was dead. I began to see that I was just like an alcoholic who can only stay sober by never taking that first drink. I can only stay mentally sober if I stay away from the "stinking thinking" that is the source of my ills.

For me, the source of mental illness lies in resentment and its Siamese twin, self-pity. Vince, a long-time AA member, explained to me that resentment is anger rethought. That is a truism. I often get angry. And so long as I walk away from my anger I am all right. But the minute I start to chew my anger over in my mind, and rethink it from every angle, my anger becomes resentment. And resentment opens the door to self-pity. And those twin evils are the root of everything that is evil in me. From self-pity I immediately branch out into selfishness, hate, greed, envy, self-doubt, and many other ills that are too numerous and embarrassing to mention.

What are my goals in this life? I guess my primary goal is to not have any goals. But, being human, I find this difficult. So I satisfy my humanity by defining them as serenity, peace of mind, and abundant living. Wow! But not impossible. Each day that I practice the twelve steps of Emotions Anonymous I come closer to those goals. I know I will never achieve them completely. But now I have a little of each almost every day of my life. And the effect on myself and those around me is amazing. I am no longer destructive to myself and my family. My peace is becoming their peace too. I no longer live a nightmare of tension all day and hesitantly go to a sleep made torment with nightmares all night.

And as I make spiritual progess, I have been slowly giving up the neurotic process of overcontrolling my life. You see, as I progressed down my various neurotic paths I slowly gave up believing in anything and everything. This caused a terrible burden. For as I lost belief in God and in people, I had to take over more and more of the burdens of controlling my world. My primary belief became a belief that if I did not have control of myself and everyone around me, disaster would soon overwhelm me. And it did. Like Job in the Bible, what I feared came to pass. And the total exhaustion of running my world destroyed me. But from the ashes I discovered God, and I willingly returned His world to Him, and that was the beginning of serenity.

To try to sum up in my own way: God is truly in His

Heaven, and I His daughter here on earth receive an abundance of His gifts each day of my life. These gifts have gotten me through times that have tried my soul, and made me stronger with each trial, and now my trials reinforce my belief in a Higher Power instead of flooding me with hate and doubt.

So thank God for my Higher Power and the twelve steps of Emotions Anonymous. Jackie has found a home.

15

Jess and Jackie

It seems to us that in life there is a largely unrecognized therapy system. We call it Mutual Need Therapy. Vince calls it the laws of life. We believe it is a set of laws and a set of relationships that each of us must spend our life discovering for ourselves so that more and more as we go through life we can truly live free with a happy heart.

While each of us must make and confirm these discoveries for ourselves, we can benefit from another's experiences. We don't need to make every mistake ourselves.

While each of us is different and while each of us has our own different view of reality (which deserves the deepest respect), there is still an ultimate reality and an ultimate lawfulness. If I am lost in the woods with a group of people, I don't want us to decide which way is north by taking a vote. I would rather we try to find which side of the trees the moss is on. Even though the clouds might hide the sun all the time we were lost, we could still try to read the signs, however dim, and act on those clues.

What is Mutual Need Therapy?

We believe you and I cannot live alone.

We believe that unless we have real communication with other people our life is so dry that we die inside and usually die physically earlier than normal.

We believe that there can be no real communication between two people unless they recognize their mutual need for each other. I need you.

We believe that before we can recognize our mutual need for each other, we need to see that there is something outside ourselves, some kind of Power higher than us. It can be a belief in anything outside ourselves, whatever we may call it, such as nature, the order we see in the universe, or even a group of people.

We believe that we give meaning to our lives to the degree we concentrate on the process of living instead of results, goals, or fulfillment.

We believe that we are physical, emotional, and spiritual beings and that unless all three functions are recognized we cannot develop fruitfully.

We believe that physical, emotional, and spiritual development is the point of life and is a lifelong process that is never completed. It is never a matter of a return to some earlier time when we were whole or complete and then lost it or had it taken away. Neither the young nor the old will lead us out of the darkness. Rather, we shall lead each other, paying proper respect to those who show us through their actions that we should give attention to their lives whether they are young or old.

We believe that we must not judge any other person and his efforts. Ideally, we would not even be aware of what we might see as his harmfulness or faltering. Our awareness of what we see as other people's problems distracts us from finding our own way.

We believe that once we have admitted to the idea of some Higher Power we need to attempt to be guided by that Power in whatever way we see it working in our lives.

We believe that while relationship with a Higher Power is crucial to our spiritual development, for our emotional and physical development we need to love and be loved by human beings.

We believe that our family is the first source of satisfying our mutual needs. If that is not the case, then we should find what the problems are in our family and attempt as hard as we can to correct them.

We believe our relationships outside the family, including our work, must enhance or support the family and at least not conflict with the family relationships. In case of conflict, it should most always be resolved in favor of the family.

We believe each member of the family should have as equal rights as humanly possible. Resentment and bad feeling in the family is usually a sign that adequate consideration has not been given to a member of the family.

We believe that each individual in the family needs to have mutual relationships outside the family for his development as a complete human being. This growth of the members of the family also feeds back into the family and strengthens it. A relationship outside the family that hurts the family is usually a sign that something is wrong with that relationship.

We believe a family is any group of related or non-related individuals who feel a responsibility and a deep commitment to each other until death and who do not make that responsibility and commitment dependent on the actions of the individuals in the family. (Even though you murder my mother or father you are still my brother —blood brother or brother by a mutually expressed agreement.)

We believe that each of us was made as a precious, unique individual full of the power and glory and majesty that is us.

We believe that being human means being imperfect. Only a God can be perfect. So we need to accept our imperfections and realize that the reason we were given our own particular set of imperfections is a mystery we must accept, and know we can never understand.

We believe that while we must accept what we are and while we cannot change what we are we can change the things we do and so we have a large degree of control over our lives through the control of our actions.

We believe that an acceptance of ourselves as we are frees us to become the more ideal self we see within, even though this can mean deliberately side-stepping other parts of ourselves that we recognize as ourselves but choose not to live out. (I see within me the potentiality to be an alcoholic or a sex maniac. I choose not to be that part of me because of its destructiveness for the rest of me and the way it would make me incapable of meeting a fuller range of my needs.)

We believe that our freedom comes from the wide range of potentialities open to us. Basic to this freedom is our freedom to make mistakes and to fail. We need our mistakes and failures to grow. How and when we grow must be left up to us. Our freedom to fail must be complete and even if it seems our failures are destructive enough to kill us we must have the freedom to grow or die. Only with the choice in our hands are we really free.

We believe there is a back-and-forth relationship as we recognize our need for other people. The love we get from them opens us more to our deeper and more ideal self. As we go deeper into our self there is more love in us to give those who need us. So we can progress in ever deepening relationships.

We believe that each of us is not everyone's cup of tea. Each of us does not vibrate on the same wave length. Only certain people will respond to our need for them. It is no disrespect to those who do not respond to us. They are right for someone else.

We believe that only when we are making an attempt to get in touch with our real self can we attract the people who can meet our real needs. When we are attempting to hide in the false self, our relationships are destructive and do not satisfy us.

We believe our unmet needs that are very strong and long-denied will often take control of us so that we seem to have no freedom from the sick games and destructive behavior those unmet needs bring us to. It usually takes some major rebuilding and some time spent meeting those needs in good ways before the need for the sick games drops away.

We believe that because of our desire to be God, we have a deep horror and fear of our human imperfections so we are more frightened of self-awareness than any other thing.

We believe that a close human relationship is like a mirror held up to us in which we see our imperfections and our limitations. Because of this, we believe people tend to avoid close relationships or take steps to destroy a relationship when they are in it. Only the experience of being loved deeply just as we are can help us manage our fear of self-awareness.

We believe love is telling how it is in our deepest heart. Nearly always this means communicating a deep sense of our own imperfection.

We believe that one of the first laws of life is give and get. To get the love we need, we must first summon up the courage to love someone else. Some of that love will be returned tenfold.

We believe that in dealing with other people the only force truly allowed us is love.

We believe that love never fails. The amount of love we are capable of in a given situation may fail, but love never fails. So often we see a new situation where there is enough love to make the difference for someone that we couldn't make.

We believe the deepest need any of us have is for each other. The only real help we can give is offering ourselves out of our need for each other. But that other person must always be completely free to need us back and must never feel our love as a burden. If there is a feeling of being burdened or imprisoned because of love, then it isn't love.

The goal of Mutual Need Therapy is to grow and develop toward that more ideal self we dimly see in us by means of mutually satisfying and continually deepening human relationships with the people around us. Physical, emotional, and spiritual difficulties will come to us as a part of our human condition, but they will often be created by us because of our unwillingness or our inability to see some law of life operating. We cannot live out of harmony with life, so we need our mistakes to show us how to bring our lives back in harmony with ourselves and life, or we will die emotionally, spiritually, or physically.

Mutual Need Therapy is a self-directed, lifelong process of moving toward a deeper realization of your more ideal self and the mutually satisfying relationships that help that process and are a result of the process.

We are Jackie and Jess. We are, with the help of our Higher Power, working on our problems. For us to grow, we need our family and the people in this community who need us back. May you find the strength and courage to build your family and your community five minutes at a time using the plea we frequently find so necessary—"Hey, God, what should I do now?"

MASTER NOVELISTS

CHESAPEAKE   CB 24163 $3.95
by James A. Michener

An enthralling historical saga. It gives the account of different generations and races of American families who struggled, invented, endured and triumphed on Maryland's Chesapeake Bay. It is the first work of fiction in ten years to be first on *The New York Times Best Seller List.*

THE BEST PLACE TO BE   PB 04024 $2.50
by Helen Van Slyke

Sheila Callaghan's husband suddenly died, her children are grown, independent and troubled, the men she meets expect an easy kind of woman. Is there a place of comfort? a place for strength against an aching void? A novel for every woman who has ever loved.

ONE FEARFUL YELLOW EYE   GB 14146 $1.95
by John D. MacDonald

Dr. Fortner Geis relinquishes $600,000 to someone that no one knows. Who knows his reasons? There is a history of threats which Travis McGee exposes. But why does the full explanation live behind the eerie yellow eye of a mutilated corpse?

8002